You're Never Too Old To Become Young

**A Revolutionary Approach On
How To Reverse the Aging Process**

David John Carmos Ph.D.

Dr. Shawn Miller

Copyright © 2006

David John Carmos & Dr. Shawn Miller

ISBN# 978-0-9725488-0-7

published by

Dragon Phoenix Productions

Library of Congress catalogue
number in Publication Data

Carmos-Miller Anti-Density Theory®
Anti-Density Theory®

Photos of Drs. Shawn Miller & David Carmos,

by Ron McFee,

Shawn Miller and David Carmos

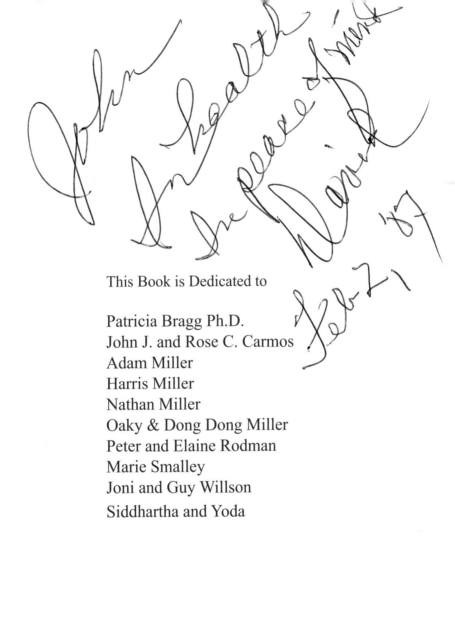

This Book is Dedicated to

Patricia Bragg Ph.D.
John J. and Rose C. Carmos
Adam Miller
Harris Miller
Nathan Miller
Oaky & Dong Dong Miller
Peter and Elaine Rodman
Marie Smalley
Joni and Guy Willson
Siddhartha and Yoda

Introduction

I was raised in an atmosphere of health. From my earliest remembrance I was imbued with ideas and concepts which instilled in me how important it is to be aware of, as my father Paul C. Bragg would say, "Living in an ageless, painless, tireless body." Over the years I have encountered many people who talk the talk, yet often they do not walk their talk. Occasional I encounter someone who so totally personifies this ideal that whenever I meet them, they are improving in every imaginable way.

These two are Dr. David Carmos and Dr. Shawn Miller. My father Paul Bragg opened the first health food store in America in 1912, and introduced such as Clint Walker, Clint Eastwood, Gloria Swanson, Robert Cummings and Jack LaLanne to natural health and nutritional concepts, and started David Carmos in lecturing in 1964. David and Shawn are the personification of what my father and I project as the ideal of health.

Dr. Shawn although younger in years has a wealth of knowledge when it comes to natural healing. He is an inspiration to his patients, family and friends. His wife and parents who are both students of his, are the picture of health. Along with his chiropractic practice in Pacific Beach, California, he lifts weights, surfs, meditates, practices yoga, lectures, writes, and is always open to growing and helping others to grow.

When my father introduced me to David in 1964, he was studying to be a priest. Shortly after that, he left the seminary, and while continuing his college in California, he began teaching yoga in Beverly Hills, and after two years at that, he then taught at Boston University for four years designing therapy, before resigning to become the Director of an historical house and museum.

David and I have stayed close over the years, and I tell him every time I see him how ageless he is. He has had an immense personal loss, yet he has come through even stronger than before. I cannot say enough in praise of these two, who truly know how to reverse the process of aging. Together, they have created a encyclopedia of health, healing and rejuvenation.

Patricia Bragg Ph.D.
January 27, 2006.

Preface I

I have had a growing interest in anti-aging for quite some time. When I see experts on rejuvenation, most seem to be saying the same thing. "Your body isn't producing super-oxide dismutase or testosterone or estrogen, as it did when you were younger, and so you must supplement these elements and then you will become younger." The exponents of this philosophy, usually don't think, look or act any younger than the average person their chronological age. Supplementation is fine as far as it goes, but it is only one aspect of how to reverse the process of aging.

Supplementing the missing elements does little to re-vitalize the body processes which will allow the body to reactivate a state of aliveness, that is both natural and normal.

It seems logical that if progressing through the aging process limits our ability to produce essential body constituents, then reversing the aging process would be to progressively move toward placing the body in a state where it will begin to manufacture these elements again.

When we consider the fact that there is no one cell in the body more than a year old, and that every cell in our body will be completely renewed within a seven year period, why age?

I personally have been working on a totally natural way to reversing or at bare minimum slow down this pattern which is so prevalent in most every society. I am my own best example of what I know to be true and live by. When I encountered Dr. Shawn Miller in April of 1998, and began to share my concepts with him, it wasn't very long before we realized our ideas and goals coincided. Together we have enhanced our personal concepts of how to reverse the process of aging. Environment certainly helps in any anti-aging process, but most every other aspect of aging, which is not due to chronology, but lifestyle, is controllable by all of us.

In the following sections of this book *You're Never Too Old To Become Young*, we will explore all those facets which will lead our readers to understand the concept that you are never too young to become old, and once by the health bug you are stung, You're Never Too Old To Become Young.

David John Carmos, San Diego, Ca. February 1, 2006

Preface II

In oneself lies the whole world, and if you know how to look and learn, the door is there and the keys are in your hand. The only one on earth that can give you either the key or the door to open is yourself. Many people throughout history have searched for the keys to obtain a state of perfect health, harmony and balance. Socrates stated that "To learn the secrets of the universe, study yourself." We are made of the same energy and matter as the Universe. We are essentially a mini universe or microcosm. As we learn the patterns in and of nature, we can have a better understanding of the world that we inhabit.

Life is always working towards creating a state of balance and harmony.This state is homeostasis. Many people work for years trying to create harmony in their life. Most often looking outside themselves for all the answers. Our life's experience is in direct proportion to our inner health. Imbalance in health leads to an imbalanced life. Your outer world mirrors your inner world. If your health is abundant and balanced, then your life is too. If your health and body feels out of balance, then your life is also.

I have often told my patients that no matter what type of symptoms are being expressed by someone, no matter how complex the scenario of dis-eases is, it can mean only one thing, and that is, something in the body is out of balance. So the only thing left is to do is find out the areas that are out of balance and start working towards creating balance in them. As we apply the laws and patterns of nature, we can recognize those areas and work towards harmonizing them.

What most people are searching for in life is not the meaning of life, but the experiences of life. The body is the vehicle in which we obtain this experience. If your body has become rusted and worn out, it is time to rejuvenate it and stop driving around an old 'junker' and instead restore and repair your vehicle to classic form and vintage status. Remember: It is never too late to be what you might have been!

Remember the message in the Tortoise and the Hare, "Slow and steady wins the race." Enjoy the process of discovery and the journey to health and self. The Turkish have a saying: "However far you've gone down the wrong road - turn back!"

A special thanks to my teacher, David Carmos.

With love always and in all ways,

Dr. Shawn Miller, February 2, 2006

Table of Contents

List of Illustrations

Anti-Density Theory

Anti-Density Theory

This chapter is uniquely different from the others in this book because unlike those aspects that can be researched, this chapter is a mixture of fact and theory. This is the authors own personal philosophy of how and why the human body ages as it does. Because of it's very nature, we will explore, observe and research the human body partly from an empirical standpoint. This was the traditional approach to learning in ancient times, and we feel that for this particular subject, it is the most logical and clearest cut approach to understanding why the body ages.

At times this way might seem a bit platitudinous, but bear with us and we are sure that this concept of aging, which to the best of our knowledge will be unlike any you have ever before heard, will be found to be so utterly simple and unique, there will be no way to deny it.

All Life Is Motion

To begin with, all life is motion. Without motion there is no life. Life diminishes in proportion to the lack of motion involved, or put more simply, what you don't use, you will tend to lose. As we progress through the aging process, our lives will gradually become more and more limited. Hence we begin to use phrases like "I can't do that any more, I'm just not as young as I use to be."

From an observational standpoint, as we behold and observe a child, it becomes quite clear that children are open and flexible. This means from

Section One -Anti-Density Theory

a mental and emotional aspect as well as from a physical one. A baby will grasp it's feet with both hands, and then place one or both in his or her mouth. A baby is always open, both wide eyed and open mouthed, and ready to receive. As opposed to this, as we become aware of our aging, the first aspect we notice in ourselves or others, is that we are beginning to lose our flexibility.

We may attempt to pick up something off the floor, and feel a tightening at our low back, thinking, "I must be getting old, that's not as easy as it used to be". The same as losing physical flexibility is a sign of aging, losing our mental or emotional flexibility is also a sign of the aging process. We use the word "process" because that is exactly what it is. It is an important realization that age is chronology, while aging is lifestyle. About now you might be thinking, "I can reflect back and see people who were never flexible, physically, mentally or emotionally". This is because they were already aging when you first encountered them. The aging process can begin at any point, no matter what our chronological age is.

"L Street Beach" - Boston

Back in the late fifties and early sixties one of your authors had the opportunity to learn from, study and observe an amazing group of men in Boston, Massachusetts. These men were chronologically in their late sixties, seventies, eighties and a few even in their nineties. They were medical physicians, lawyers, teachers and just average business men before retirement. Yet years before, many of them were

Section One - Anti-Density Theory

headliners in the Keith circuit, the best entertainment touring circuit in all of vaudeville. They had been hand-balancers, jugglers and/or acrobats in their earlier years, and they had kept up the practice of these skills even into their retirement years.

As I watched and learned from them, I began to notice that they all had one unique trait. Everyone of them was physically, mentally and emotionally open. Not one of them was closed to a new idea. Most of them had lost some of their youthful vigor, yet there was still a spark that just jumped out, and was so clearly defined that it was impossible to ignore. Many of these men were also " L Street Brownies".

Boston's Muscle Beach

For more than a hundred years the city of Boston has operated a beach which was really the east coast version of California's world famous Muscle Beach, but Boston's version existed long before California's Muscle Beach got it's name. L Street Beach had exercise equipment, including weights, chinning bars, a measured walking/track area, an indoor solarium with special quartz glass to allow in the ultra-violet rays of the sun, even during those cold Boston winters, and there was a set of parallettes, which is a foot high version of the parallel bars a gymnast would use. These were utilized for hand balancing.

The reason these men were called the "L Street Brownies", is because they were tanned year round; not the easiest thing to do in Boston. The event the "Brownies" are best known for is their annual New Years Day swim in the Atlantic Ocean, where they

Section One - Anti-Density Theory

have to break the salt water ice in order to enter the water. At one time I was the youngest of the "Brownies". This was from the time I was nineteen until I was twenty-seven.

There were fences on the beach that were built out into the ocean water. Between the fences was one-eighth of a mile; which was helpful to measure distances when swimming or jogging. One day while I was running along the beach, I passed one of these men, a long time friend named Jake. As I ran by this 84 year young athlete doing a fast-paced walk, I called out, "Are you doing a mile?" Jake's reply was, "Nope just a smile!" I called back "What's a smile?" His reply was "One fence." One sign of health is a good sense of humor. Another is a quick wit. The reason for this is, a person that is open sees possibilities that a person who is less open, either totally misses or refuses to look at.

Why God Has So Few Friends

A great line I have always had an affinity to, since I first heard it, is a quote from the autobiography of St. Theresa of Avila, a fifteenth century Spanish mystic. She would compose her own prayers on the spur of the moment. One story she mentions is while riding on a mule by a stream, the mule saw a serpent and suddenly balked, sending her flying through the air, and landing in the stream. At this point she looked into the heavens declaring "Oh God, I realize why you have so few friends, when you treat the ones you have the way you do". Another of her prayers which is perfect to demonstrate our point is "Oh Lord, deliver us from sour faced saints". When a person is healthy, they should be happy.

At another time I ran into another long time friend Al Peckham. Al had been an executive with a utility company in Boston. He was vegetarian, and he had raised his children to be vegetarian too. Al loved to wrestle, and he taught his sons to wrestle also. In fact one of his sons Jim, was in the 1956 Olympics as a Graeco-Roman wrestler. Jim later became the Olympic Graeco-Roman wrestling coach for the United States in the 1984 Olympics. After retirement, Al had moved to Beverly Hills, California, and I had not seen him in several years.

The Cyclist

One day I ran into him on L Street Beach. He asked if I would do him a favor. He said that he had a project he wanted to take on and needed a little advice. He further explained that over the years he had developed the typical injuries that a wrestler ends up with, including knee and ankle problems. He asked if I would design a program for him to help strengthen his knees and ankles, and to develop flexibility in them.

I put together a yoga program for him, and put him through it two or three times, until he got it down, and then he returned to California, and I never saw him again. About six months later I ran into one of the guys at the beach and he said "Did you hear about Al Peckham?" Thinking the worst I said, "No, what happened?" The man replied, "Al just rode his bicycle from Beverly Hills to Boston."

Section One - Anti-Density Theory

He had accomplished his goal. At the time Al was about 82 years of age.

As we go through the aging process one of the first things we begin to develop is attitude. This involves the way we carry on, hold our head, stride when we walk, etc. This is done for any number of reasons. One reason is to make ourselves appear sophisticated, and so that we project an air of confidence.

Unfortunately, attitudes tend to lock up our physical structure. As a result, instead of being ourselves we begin to act out a role of what we want to project to others. Some people never stop doing this throughout their entire life.

What Is Health?

Another very important point is to define what true health really is. We in the United States are raised to believe that health is the absence of symptoms. That is not necessarily so. Picture an older person who might be on ten to fifteen medications a day. They may be taking twenty-five to thirty pills daily and although they are not showing any symptoms, they are anything but healthy.

Their lungs might be full of phlegm, or in some other way may not be working properly, they have chronic aches and pains, ongoing digestive problems and their bowels have not worked well in years. During the night when they should be quiet and resting they are tossing and turning in their sleep. This level of existence is so widespread, it is often considered normal. During the day time when they should be

Section One - Anti-Density Theory

active they are dragging themselves through the day by bouncing from one stimulant to the next, often in the form of coffee or chocolate, both of which are loaded with caffeine or by eating some simple forms of sugar for a quick fix. Every stimulant has after it's initial action, an opposite and equal reaction, so the result is, the energy drops.

The Symptomatic Approach To Health

Unfortunately, the main healing modality in the United States is based on symptomatic treatment. When a person has a headache, that is a symptom. To treat the symptom isn't wrong, but to do that only and not work at removing the cause is. It's like having a beautiful building, with a state of the art alarm system, and when the alarm goes off, to warn you of the danger inside, doing something to deaden the warning, while ignoring the fire, with the expectation that the cause will just disappear.

The cause of a headache may be from many things including stress, constipation, a subluxation or vertebral mal-alignment of the spine, high blood pressure, diet, and the numeration goes on almost ad infinitum, listing a myriad of causes. If all we ever do is treat symptoms through medication, and never work on removing the causes, how can we ever expect to become healthy?

How Does the Body Work?

Let's take a quick look at how the body works. There is no cell in the body more than a year old. Some cells last longer than others. Some last ninety days, while others last one-hundred and twenty

Section One - Anti-Density Theory

days; but within a seven year period, every cell you now have in your body will be completely renewed. That is standard physiology. Now, what are our cells made of? They are made of the way we move, talk, eat, drink, think, breathe, act and react. When you consider the aspects of which we as humans are composed, and the brief length of time within which these cells survive, if every cell within our body will be completely renewed within a seven year period, and if we have control over the aspects of which our cells are composed, why should we age?

Variations Within Aspects

One difference comes in the way we nourish our cells. Now by that we do not mean only the nutritional aspects, but beyond that the quality of what we take in, as it applies to the age of the food and the conditions under which it was grown, and even over that, the ability of our body to break down, rearrange, transform, absorb and eliminate what we are taking into our systems. Many people have chronic digestive disturbances and over the years, they have only treated the symptom, and never done a thing to remove the cause.

Personal Level of Health

Unfortunately, we are programmed through advertising, our own ignorance, our parents and friends, and often our primary care givers, to just buy an over the counter remedy, imbibe it, and then go happily along our way. Often when people give free advice on health, they have no concept of what they are saying, and although they may mean well,

Section One - Anti-Density Theory

usually they have no idea what they are talking about when it comes to real health. To most people "sick" is when they cannot get out of bed or when they have to be hospitalized. When you are constipated, your sinuses are blocked, you are diabetic, arthritic, or have migraines, in reality you are not really healthy. If you still insist on thinking of yourself as healthy, it would be at best a modicum level of health. This is a level of health where many people will say "Hey, I may not be great, but I'm getting by". Take away their daily intake of digestive tablets, headache pills, anti-histamines, pain killers and the like and see just how good they feel then.

The Standard American Diet

Another aspect to consider is the Standard American Diet. This is a standard based in part on commercial interest. If you want to get an idea of what you will feel like by living on it, just take a look at the acronym it forms, and that should open your eyes a little. The United States is generally conceded to be the most affluent nation on this planet. Yet we are forty-eighth in health when compared to the other nations of the earth. Ethnic aspects have been considered, but America is such a kaleidoscope of nationalities, it is clear that the answer does not lie there. When we look at the health levels of several poorer countries, many have relatively low incidences of the degenerative and killer diseases such as heart disease, cancer and stroke.

Cornell University Studies

The work of Colin Campbell Ph.D. of Cornell

Section One - Anti-Density Theory

University, concern his studies in China, exploring why in less affluent and technologically undeveloped countries, the incidences of the three killer diseases of the industrialized nations are either extremely low or practically non-existent. These studies revealed that in such atmospheres, the population subsists on lots of locally grown, unsprayed, unprocessed foods of a vegetable or grain origin.[1] Such foods contain the recently discovered phytochemicals known to be found only in vegetables, fruits and whole grains.

These are elements that fight the growth of cancer in the body.[2] These cultures consume flesh in minimal amounts not because they are necessarily health minded, but because they use their animals for beasts of burden, or because they cannot afford to eat a lot of flesh, or because they have no way of preserving forms of protein that are in a state of putrefaction. In most primitive cultures, whole grains such as rice, wheat or corn and legumes such as soy, peas or some other type of bean, form the mainstay of the eating regimen.

Traditional Chinese Diet

It was found that at breakfast, lunch and dinner, whole grains, vegetables and fruit, make up the mainstay of their diet. Flesh foods are consumed in small quantities. Their sodium intake high, but their food is loaded with the phytochemicals and fiber and little of their food is processed. It is fresh from their own gardens, it has no chemical growth stimulators or pesticides, very little oil is used, and it is loaded with sprouts, which are extremely important.

Section One - Anti-Density Theory

Diet of Southern Italy

The same research study showed that in southern Italy, the diet is rich in pasta, vegetables, seafood and olive oil. In southern Italy heart disease along with breast and colon cancer are much lower than in the United States and Canada. Instead of white bread and butter they use whole grain crackers with fruit preserves.[3] Most of the grocery shopping is done at outdoor markets where the local farmers sell fresh produce. Flesh is generally in the form of fish; baked or broiled, but not fried. They rarely use cream sauces or fatty cheeses in their food preparation. Comparing the three cultures and their totally different diet regimens, on an average, the total number of calories from fat in the American diet is about 37% as compared to a low of 15% in China. Southern Italians get about 30% of their total calories from fat, but in China and Italy, it is mainly unsaturated fat. Americans eat on the average about 260 grams of fruits and vegetables per day. The southern Italians eat 463 grams, and the Chinese eat 354 grams daily.[4] There are 28.5 grams to one ounce. As cultures become more affluent they tend to consume richer foodstuffs.

When we look at the percentages of the three big killers, in the United States and Canada, heart disease accounts for 46% of all deaths, cancer chronicles 21%, and stroke totals 13%. That means that 80% of all deaths in the United States and Canada are the result of these three conditions. Dr. Campbell's research showed that the men of China have 25% the cancer rate of American men, and

Section One - Anti-Density Theory

Chinese women die of breast cancer at a rate only 16% that of American women.

Coronary Arteries

The human heart has two arteries which branch off from the heart to supply the heart itself with blood. These are only about an inch long, and look somewhat like elbow macaroni. If one of these arteries is blocked off, that part of the heart ceases to function. This is known as a myocardial infarction or heart attack. In the United States one occurs every 25 seconds. Most people die during their first attack. In the United States another person dies every 45 seconds as the result of a heart attack. Often there is never any advanced warning.

Atheroma

The cause of this blockage is known as atherosclerosis, which is a narrowing of the arteries due to a buildup inside the artery, resulting from saturated fat and cholesterol. These fatty deposits which buildup in layers are called atheromas or plaques. When they become advanced the fatty contents will often rupture into the artery and form a clot. A stroke is the same thing, but in the brain.

As the blood vessels move further away from the heart, in order to maintain homeostasis or adjusted pressure, the walls of the blood vessels become narrower and thinner. They also tend to become more brittle. After a stroke, the part of the brain involved goes dormant. The standard teaching is that, that part of the brain dies. Yet in work conducted by one of your authors in Mexico, electrical acupuncture was able to restore at least partial function in a minimum number of treatments, on the thirty or so stroke victims on whom it was applied. Although the human body manufactures small amounts of cholesterol for it's own needs, the only dietary source of cholesterol is found in animal products. Saturated fat in nature occurs in only a few vegetable items. These are palm kernel oil, cocoa butter and coconut. The dietary sources are meat, dairy products and eggs.[5]

Research Results

Now let us look at some of the research which has long been available concerning these three. As reported in Circulation as well as by the Harvard University Press, Dr. Ansel Keys, who at the time fifty years ago, was with the University of Minnesota, School of Public Health, conducted a seven country study.[6] He began the study after noticing the rising incidence of heart disease among middle aged men. It involved more than 12,000 men in Japan, the Netherlands, Yugoslavia, Finland, Greece, Italy and the United States.

The purpose of the study was to analyze the possible role of diet in relationship to heart disease. Finland and the United States had the highest consumption of cholesterol and saturated fat, and also had the highest death rate from heart disease. Dr. Keys, one of the foremost nutrition researchers in the world, has been involved in nutrition research for so long, it was he that the famous "K" rations of the armed services during the Second World War were designed by and named for.

Section One - Anti-Density Theory

Framingham Heart Study

Around the time Dr. Keys began his research, another study was begun in Framingham, Massachusetts, in which nearly 5,000 men and women have been studied. Dr Richard Havel of the University of California during an interview for the MacNeil Lehrer Report stated, "The Framingham study has been a landmark study in identifying the precursors for coronary heart disease. The three salient factors in particular, were cigarette smoking, high blood cholesterol and high blood pressure . The latter two are related in part to diet."[7]

By the early '70s, the Framingham study, the Ansel Keys study and the Colin Campbell study had reached similar conclusions. This was simply that those populations who had high levels of heart disease and breast and colon cancer all consumed high percentages of saturated fats and cholesterol laden foods; little of fruits, vegetables & whole grains.

Dr. M.G. Marmot - U.C. Berkeley

Dr. M.G. Marmot of the University of California at Berkeley, in a study published in the American Journal of Epidemiology, revealed the results of a research program which consisted of men of Japanese ancestry.[8] The subjects involved were living in several parts of the world. The men were catalogued in groups, and classified according to their intake of saturated fat and cholesterol and deaths due to coronary heart disease. Japan has a high incidence of smoking but a low intake of animal fat. They also have a low incidence of cancer and heart disease.

Section One - Anti-Density Theory

The National Academy of Sciences

The National Academy of Sciences Study and the Surgeon General's Report came to similar conclusions. The director of the National Academy of Sciences Report and the senior advisor for the Surgeon General's Report, was Dr. Susha Palmer. She has stated, "The findings of a single study mean very little. In our reports we examined nearly 10,000 studies and when several well documented studies pointed in the same direction, we used them as a basis for determining conclusions. That is the kind of consensus that the public needs to pay attention to, rather than the dramatic headlines of single experiments."[9]

In general the two reports concluded that "... a diet high in saturated fat and cholesterol is a major factor in contributing to heart disease, and a diet high in total fat contributes to several kinds of cancer. The intake of vegetables, whole grains and fruits are associated with low levels of certain types of cancer as well as several other types of disease."[10]

Dr. Dean Ornish

At present the standard American Heart Association recommendation is that no more than 30% of the total caloric intake should be in the form of fat. We the authors, consider that percentage to be far too high. It would be wiser to stay closer to 10-15% of total caloric intake in the form of fat, and even then, limit the intake to unsaturated and cholesterol free (animal free) forms of fat. Another researcher that we do agree with is Dr. Dean Ornish of the

University of California at Berkeley. Dr. Ornish has stated, "We've gotten to a point in medicine where it is considered conservative to cut people open, to put them on powerful drugs for the rest of their lives with known and unknown side effects; and it is considered somehow radical to get people to walk some, to manage stress better, to eat vegetables, and to stop smoking. I think things are a little topsy-turvy."[11] Dr. Ornish places his heart patients on a regimen of exercise, yoga and a near vegetarian diet. Fat intake is no more than 10% of total calories from fat. At the end of one year, 82% of Dr. Ornish's patients showed less blockage in their arteries.

Dr. Robert Wissler

A few years back, Dr. Robert Wissler, of the University of Chicago, published in the <u>Annals of the New York Academy of Sciences</u>, the results of a study he conducted wherein he fed a group of rhesus monkeys the standard American diet. To a second group of monkeys they fed a diet lower in calories, cholesterol and saturated fat. They then killed the monkeys and examined their arteries. Those on the standard American diet had six times as much cholesterol as those in the second group.[12]

Another monkey experiment conducted at the University of Iowa by Dr. Mark Armstrong fed the simians a regimen rich in cholesterol laden egg yolk. After their arteries had become half blocked, the amounts of cholesterol laden fats was reduced and 18 months later the atherosclerotic buildup was less than one-third what it had been on the egg yolk regimen.[13]

Section One - Anti-Density Theory

An important point to understand here is the above experiments were conducted on animals which are by nature and by structural definition, vegetarian.

Dr. William S. Collins

Conversely, at a research program under the guidance of Dr. William S. Collins and published in <u>Medical Counterpoint</u>, Dr. Collins stated, "In recent studies, many of them at my laboratory at the Maimonides Medical Center, the carnivorous animal appears to have an almost unlimited capacity to handle saturated fats and cholesterol, whereas vegetarian animals have a very restricted capacity to handle these food components. It is virtually impossible to produce atherosclerosis in the dog, even when a half pound of butter fat is added to its' meat ration. On the other hand, adding only two grams of cholesterol daily to a rabbits chow for two months produces striking fatty changes in it's arterial wall." [14]

Dr. Paul Dudley White

Dr. Paul Dudley White, who was known as the Dean of American Cardiology, and was the heart specialist for President Eisenhower when he had his heart attack, was a brilliant and humble man. He would walk and ride his bicycle through the Back Bay area of Boston, and was always very approachable. This man walked his talk. He once told one of your authors, that when he first became interested in the heart, back in 1926, other physicians laughed at him. They said, "Paul, it is only a pump, nothing more." That shows us how much things have advanced.

In 1964, Dr. White traveled to Hunzaland, in

Section One - Anti-Density Theory

the mountains near Kashmir. The Hunzas are said to be the descendants of the soldiers of Alexander the Great. They live in an isolated area of the world, and it was after these people, who were rediscovered in the early part of the 20th century, that a film based on their fabled longevity called <u>Shangri-la</u> was made.

Dr. White tested their blood pressure, blood cholesterol, and performed electro-cardiogram studies. The result was that not a trace of coronary heart disease was present. This included the twenty-five male Hunzakuts who were in their nineties.

Later upon returning to the States, Dr. White in an article published in the <u>American Heart Journal</u>, stated a possible causative connection between the Hunza diet, which contained very little flesh, but a high content of non-animal products, especially apricots, as a possible reason for their amazing level of health.[15] In fact about the only common problem among the Hunza population was a slight eye irritation due to their cooking their chapati (wafer-like bread) over an open fire, indoors.

Loma Linda University Studies

At a meeting of the <u>American Public Health Association</u> in the mid '70s and later published in the <u>American Journal of Clinical Nutrition</u>, was revealed the results of a study conducted at Loma Linda University. Loma Linda is a Seventh Day Adventist university. Seventh Day Adventist's are by religious belief mainly vegetarian, following the guidance found in Genesis 1:29. The study involved 24,000 subjects. The results showed that the heart disease mortality rates for lacto-ovo (dairy and egg) vegetarians was one-third that of those on the standard American diet. Vegan (no animal products) vegetarians (as are your authors), showed one-tenth the heart disease rate of those on the standard American diet.[16]

A similar study was conducted thirty years later by Loma Linda University, The results were published in a Fall issue of National Geographic in 2005. The results of the earlier studies held up. Time shows that truth works and Nature knows.

Time Magazine

Hold the Eggs and Butter, the famous Time magazine story where on the cover was a simulation of a face using two fried eggs for the eyes and a strip of bacon for the mouth, and where the cover story revealed the latest medical findings, stated "In regions... where meat is scarce, cardio-vascular disease is unknown."[17] The research goes on and on, and this is just on heart disease alone.

Korean War Studies

How did all this awareness begin? Back in the mid 50s, during the Korean conflict, autopsies were performed on many of the American soldiers that had been killed in the fighting. Most of these were young men 18 and 19 years of age. They were considered the best conditioned fighting men in the world, eating a rich American diet. Of those killed in the fighting and then later autopsied, it was discovered that on the average, 77% of their blood vessels had accumulated atherosclerotic deposits, and these were young and active males. Their Korean counterparts of a similar age, who had also been killed in the fighting, upon autopsy, showed no such blockage; as as reported in the Journal of the American Medical Association. During this same period the captured Korean prisoners were fed the same diet as the American soldiers. In no time at all, their blood cholesterol levels shot up to a significant level.[18] Such a buildup inevitably leads to atherosclerosis.

Most Common Forms of Cancer

The Conquest of Cancer Act, signed by then President Nixon in 1971, was the beginning of the national war on cancer. The most common forms of cancer, are of the lung, breast, colon, prostate, pancreas and ovary. According to articles published in the British Medical Journal, the New England Journal of Medicine, the Journal of the American Medical Association, the Department of Health, Education and Welfare, and the Select Committee On Nutrition and Human Needs, the death rate from these cancers has either stayed the same or increased over the past 50 years.[19]

National Cancer Institute

In 1985, Dr. John Bailar, the former editor of the Journal of the National Cancer Institute, which organization, he had been connected with for twenty-five years, said that today more people are being included in the statistics to make things appear that more victims of cancer are being cured, as was reported in Animals Agenda.[20] Another definition for a cancer cure is that if a patient survives five years from the day he or she is diagnosed, then they are

Section One - Anti-Density Theory

cured of cancer. People are becoming aware of their eating habits, their exercise, their bodies in general, and are living with a greater awareness than in the past. Every 30 seconds another is diagnosed with cancer in the United States. Every 55 seconds another person dies of cancer in the United States. These numbers are way too high. The average amount a patient pays is $25,000.[21]

U.S. Senate Study on Nutrition

In 1977 the Select Committee on Nutrition and Human Needs of the United States Senate published it's findings. It's chair, Senator George McGovern said, "The chances of being cured of cancer in the United States are not significantly better than they were back in 1940." He referred to the fight against cancer as a "multi-billion dollar medical failure."[22] Senator McGovern asked the director of the National Cancer Institute what percentage of cancers are caused by diet? The head of the largest cancer institute in the world said, "Up to 50%."[23] From a purely business standpoint, there is far more money to be made in treatment than in prevention.[24]

Cancer Research Studies

In the book Advances In Cancer Research, the author Peter Chowka states, "At present we have an overwhelming evidence that none of the risk factors for cancer is...more significant than diet and nutrition.[25] In an article published in Vegetarian Times, Dr. Gio B. Gori is quoted telling the U.S. Congress, "Nutrition science is about to be coming of age........no

Section One - Anti-Density Theory

other field of research seems to hold better promise, for the prevention and control of cancer and other illnesses, and for securing and maintaining human health. An imbalance of dietary components could lead to cancer and cardio-vascular disease. Evidence makes this not only possible, but certain. The dietary factors are principally meat and fat intake."[26]

According to the book <u>Jack Spratt's Legacy-The Science and Politics of Fat and Cholesterol</u> by Patricia Hausman, "In cancer, meat and fat intake have been increasingly implicated."[27] Dr. Mark Hegstead of Harvard University was asked by the Federal Trade Commission concerning the diet and cancer connection and he replied, "I think it is clear that the American diet is indicated as a cause of heart disease; and it is pertinent I think to point out, the same diet is now found in many forms of cancer; breast cancer, colon cancer and others."[28] As published in <u>Preventive Medicine</u> and the <u>Journal of the National Cancer Institute</u>, researchers were finding that cancer is high where meat consumption is high, and low where meat consumption is low.

Cancer and Food Intake

Statistically there is not a single population in the world where high meat intake does not equal high cancer rate. The meat industry countered this very clear evidence by saying that it was genetic factors that caused cancer and heart disease.[29] Even now into the 21st century, the common cry for many of the conditions that cannot be quelled by medical science is "genes". Genes do have a roll, but not to the point where we do not have control over our overall health. The <u>National Cancer Institute</u> through Dr. John Berg, conducted a study which correlated nearly 200 foods with colon cancer rates. As reported in their Journal, the intake of meat was the most closely associated with colon cancer. Another factor included in this study was the intake of fat.[30] The <u>American Journal of Digestive Diseases</u> and the <u>Journal of Pathology</u> published articles by Hill and Hepner respectively. In effect these articles said, the digestion of meat itself, produces strong carcinogenic substances in the colon, and meat eaters must produce extensive bile acids in the intestines to deal with the meat they eat, particularly deoxycholic acid, which is converted by the clostridia bacteria in our intestines into powerful carcinogens (cancer causing agents).[31]

When Cholesterol Doesn't Show Up

Some people intake high levels of cholesterol but don't show it in their blood tests. Most people will carry the cholesterol deposits in their arteries which can eventually lead to heart disease. On occasion science encounters a person, whose system sends the cholesterol deposits to their intestinal tract. These people have high levels of cholesterol in the intestine and high rates of cancer of the colon, as reported in the <u>New England Journal of Medicine</u>.[32]

Japanese Studies

The largest studies ever conducted on cancer were done by Dr. Takeshi Hirayama at the National Cancer Research Institute in Tokyo. More than 120,000 persons have been monitored for decades.

In one study women were checked for breast cancer in relation to their intake of cheese, eggs, butter and meat. The conclusions were that those who eat meat on a daily basis, face a rate of cancer four times that of those who ate little to no meat. The more fat containing foods like butter, cheese and eggs, the greater the risk of breast cancer, as published in the Journal of the National Cancer Institute.[33]

As reported in the Canadian Medical Association Journal, Dr. Ronald Phillips mentions in Cancer Research that the evidence is that "Vegetarian diets strongly reduce the incidence of uterine, breast, colon, and ovarian cancers."[34] As reported in Lancet, "Atherosclerosis tends to reduce the blood flow to our other organs as well as the heart, often resulting in impotence."[35]

Years of Buildup

It is one thing to eliminate additional saturated fats and cholesterol, it is another however, to be able to eradicate all of the elements such as the saturated fat and cholesterol deposits that have been storing up in your system over the years. One aspect that must be stressed is that along with changing the type of fat which we take in is to cut way back on all types of fat, and this includes even the oils. The difference between a fat and an oil is the amount of saturation.

Differences In Saturation

As a carbon chain compound fills in the valences, which are places for various chemical elements to attach, the compound becomes more saturated. The result is, oils become solid at room temperature. If we had three cups, each containing a different kind of heated fat, one filled with bacon fat, one with olive oil, and the other filled with soy or safflower oil, they would all be in a liquid state. If we allowed these to sit at room temperature for a few hours, the olive and soy oils would remain in a liquid state. The bacon fat however would have solidified. If we then placed all three in a refrigerated atmosphere for another hour, then the olive oil would also solidify. The reason for this is that while the soy oil is very unsaturated, the olive oil contains a medium level of saturation and the bacon fat is very saturated.

Anti-Density Theory

Along with the facts that have already been revealed through the intake of saturated fat and cholesterol, being unquestionably connected with the three greatest killers in our culture, is there anything else that the intake of animal fats can lead to? Yes! That is the aging of our bodies. The reason for this is the increase in the density of our tissue.

What are the Signs of Youth?

If we observe a child, no matter what the age, we will see that a child is always flexible. A baby will play with it's body, double itself in all manner of positions, and grasping it's feet, pull them into it's mouth. Being open and supple is the way of youth. If we observed a child who was lacking in flexibility, we would know that something is not right with that child. As we progress through the aging process, a very clear pattern begins to form. We begin to lose our flexibility. It matters not whether that loss is on a mental, physical or emotional level. It is a sure sign of the aging process taking over.

Internal Organ Structure

Of the main organs of the human body, one half are solid by structure and the remaining half are hollow by structure. The solid organs are the lungs, kidneys, liver, heart, pancreas, and spleen. The lungs, which are often thought of as hollow, are in reality more like a pair of sponges. The heart, although it has chambers in it, is actually a thick walled structure, which makes it a solid organ. In ancient times the pancreas and spleen were considered to be of the same energy, and consequently were looked on as a single integrated union. The structurally hollow organs are much easier to remember. They are the stomach, small intestine, large intestine, urinary bladder and gall bladder.

Function of the Internal Organs

The design of the solid organs is to absorb the blood, extract what it needs, and to either combine with or transform into, other substances within the body, and then be secreted back into the bloodstream to move on and perform their next job. This is accomplished during the dilation (or expansion), and the compression (or contraction) of the dense or solid organs. While we are chronologically and biologically young, this dilation and contraction of the tissues of the body occurs in a smooth, fluid rhythm. However, as we increase the density of our tissues, this rhythm is hindered in it's timing, as well as in it's free-flowing un-encumbered motion. Because of this

Section One - Anti-Density Theory

functional hindrance, the blood is not processed as well or as fully as it should be, the elements are not converted as efficiently as they could be, the dilation and contraction of the tissues are not as great as they ought to be, and we begin the process of aging. This may commence at any time, no matter what our chronological age is. There can be a great difference between our chronological and our biological age.

Naturally Strong Constitution

On occasion we might encounter someone who may appear to have a cast iron stomach; one who can seemingly ingest anything. The authors experience is, that this kind of individual on the surface may appear invincible, but when the day of reckoning arrives among what they imbibe, how they digest it, and how it congests them, they get hit hard. There are certain immutable laws of Nature. The basic guideline when it comes to natural law is, "Obey or pay!" In other words, even though we may think we are defying Natural law and escaping with no deleterious consequences, the only one we are fooling in the long run is ourselves. When we violate a law of Nature, even though it is done through ignorance, we still must pay the toll for our indiscretion.

Nutrition In Medical School

Yet, why is it that physicians who generally project themselves as being experts on nutrition and health, rarely bring up the kind of information we have been covering in this chapter? According to Philip Kapleau in his book To Cherish All Life, only 30 out of 125 medical schools in the United States

Section One - Anti-Density Theory

have a required course in nutrition.[36] One of the items revealed was that the average medical physician in the United States received less than three hours of training in nutrition while in medical school, as reported by John McDougall M.D. in The McDougall Plan.[37] As John Robbins points out in his Pulitzer Prize nominated book, Diet For A New America, Dr. Michelle Harrison at the 69th annual meeting of the American Medical Women's Association, in referring to nutritional training in medical school said, "They had one lecture, on a Saturday morning, and it wasn't compulsory. I don't remember what was in the lecture, because I didn't go."[38]

Taking Responsibility

So ultimately, each of us needs to take responsibility for our own lives. We are now in a new century and a new millennium. It is time to shuck off our 20th century concepts of reality and health. The opportunity has arrived to question everything we have ever been told about life, to examine all those concepts which we have been programmed to believe, to challenge everything about us that is not working in our lives. Some of our programming may work. That we keep. Many things, which we have never questioned before, should be confronted. See if those concepts can really stand on their own.

Challenge Your Programming

Now some people will say, "I cannot change." When asked "Why?", they will probably respond, "Because I was not raised that way." There are many things we are raised to do, which we never do, as well as things we were raised to never do, which we do all the time. The difference is that some things did not work in our lives and so we discarded them, and substituted things that do work. That is how we grow and evolve in life. One-hundred years ago, the only part of a woman you could see walking down the street, was her face. Everything else was covered. Later, in the "flapper" era, older generations were shocked to see shorter dresses, bare arms and exposed knees. In the mid-30s, Swing music was considered trash. In the fifties Elvis and the Beatles were considered vulgar, loud, wild and with hair that was too long. The job of the younger generation is to move beyond the older one, otherwise there is no growth. At present there is the beginning of the belief that we can slow down the aging process. The rest of this book is dedicated to how to accomplish the answer to this question that has gone unanswered throughout the millennia. The authors of this book live this anti-density theory, challenging it's precepts on a daily basis, whether working with other physicians, patients, friends, family or our own lives.

Avoid Animal Fats

At this point it should be abundantly clear that if you want to live a high quality life, as well as a long one, first avoid animal fats. Yet, there are still a lot of questions that need to be answered. These involve how to reverse this aging process which is so prevalent. What to eat to improve the quality of our health and life? How to exercise? How to lower our stress level? How to change our way of thinking? Which

Section One - Anti-Density Theory

vitamin and mineral supplements to take? Which herbals might be helpful to counteract the effects of aging that we may have already experienced? How to minimize the effects of old injuries? Finally, how to take those elements that are stored at the tissue level and draw them back into the bloodstream to be eliminated through the organs of elimination?

The Austrian Wendt Studies

About thirty years ago, a medical physician Dr. Wendt, in Austria was curious why a baby can nurse on mother's milk which is only about 5% protein, and yet become fat? We know that as people progress through the aging process, they consume large quantities of protein, yet still are malnourished, lacking energy and are often underweight. Dr. Wendt continued to study the subject as did his son and then later his grandson, all of whom are medical physicians.

Their studies eventually led them to the conclusion that the basal membrane also known as the basement membrane, is quite thin and porous on a baby. As we move through the aging process this basal membrane which separates the capillary wall from the cell wall becomes thicker and less porous. Since the nutrition consumed cannot be absorbed into the body until it is stored at the cellular level, and since this absorption occurs through the process of osmosis, once the wall thickens, only the most concentrated elements are absorbed through it, to be utilized by the body.

Osmosis by definition is the passing of a substance from a greater concentration to a lesser one

Section One - Anti-Density Theory

through a semi-permeable membrane. This study, which is now known as <u>Wendt, Wendt and Wendt</u>, found out that as the dietary regimen is changed, the wall becomes thinner. Now what do you think might be the element that caused the basal membrane to thicken? The answer that the Wendts' discovered was protein, specifically, animal protein[39]. Using the Anti-Density Theory®, the body not only becomes healthier, it also becomes leaner and more flexible; and flexibility is definitely an essential aspect of being youthful. The opposite of flexibility is contractility. As people progress through the aging process, their muscular tissue becomes either too flaccid or too tight. Either aspect without the other is an imbalance. In all, there are nine basics to a well balanced conditioning program. All this will be covered later in the chapter on body movement and rejuvenation exercises.

Dr. John J. Federkiewicz M.D. at the age of 68 years sitting on salt water ice, at "L" St. Beach, South Boston, Ma.

Section One - Anti-Density Theory

1.
Woodruff, Judy (hosted by) <u>Eat Smart</u> MacNeil-Lehrer Report, MacNeil Lehrer Productions, 1991;

2.
<u>ibid.</u>
Kirschmann, Gayla, J. and Kirschmann, John D. <u>Nutrition Almanac</u> fourth edition, McGraw-Hill, N.Y., 1996, p.31, 151;

3.
Keys, Ansel <u>Eat Smart</u> MacNeil-Lehrer Report, MacNeil Lehrer Productions, 1991;

4.
Keys, Ansel <u>ibid.</u>

5.
Robbins, John <u>Diet for A New America</u> Stillpoint Publishing, Walpole, N.H., 1987;

6.
Keys, Ansel <u>ibid.</u>
Keys, Ansel <u>Coronary Heart Disease in Seven Countries, American Heart Association Monograph #29</u> Circulation, 41, Supplement 1, 1970, p.211;
Keys, Ansel <u>Seven Countries - A Multivariate of Death and Coronary Heart Disease in Ten Years</u> Harvard University Press, Cambridge, Massachusetts, 1980;

7.
Richard Havel <u>Eat Smart</u> MacNeil-Lehrer Report (as above)

8.
Marmot, M. <u>Epidemiologic Studies of Coronary Heart Disease and Stroke in Japanese Men</u> American Journal of Epidemiology, 102:511, 1975;

9.
Palmer, Susha <u>Eat Smart</u> MacNeil Lehrer Report (as above);

10 .
Palmer, Susha, Marmot, M.G., <u>Eat Smart</u> MacNeil Lehrer Report (as above);

11.
Ornish, Dean <u>Effects of Stress Management Training and Dietary Changes in Treating Ischemic Heart Disease</u> Journal of the American Medical Association 249:54, 1983

12.
Wissler, R. <u>Studies of Regression in Advanced Atherosclerosis in Experimental Animals and Man</u> Annals of the New York Academy of Science, 275:363, 1976;

13.
Armstrong, Mark <u>Regression of Coronary Atheromatosis in Rhesus Monkeys</u> Circ Res, 27:59, 1970;

14.
Collins, William, s. <u>Atherosclerotic Disease: An Anthropologic Theory</u> Medical Counterpoint, December, 1969;

15.
White, Paul Dudley, American Heart Journal, 1964;

16.
Phillips, R. <u>Coronary Heart Disease Mortality Among Seventh Adventists with Differing Dietary Habits</u> abstract of the American Public Health Association Meeting, Chicago, November 16-20, 1975;

Section One - Anti-Density Theory

17.

Walles, C. Hold the Eggs and Butter: Cholesterol Is Proved Deadly and Our Diet May Never Be the Same Time, March 26, 1984, p.62;

18.

Enos, F. Pathogenesis of Coronary Disease of American Soldiers Killed in Korea Journal of the American Medical Association, 158:912, 1955

Collins, W. Atherosclerotic Disease: An Anthropologic Theory Medical Counterpoint, December, 1969, p.54

Taik, Lee, Kyu, Chemico-pathological Studies Archives of Internal Medicine, 109:426, 1962

Hausman, Patricia Jack Spratt's Legacy-The Science and Politics of Fat and Cholesterol Richard Marek Publishers, New York, 1981, p.28, 196;

19.

Baum, M. The Curability of Breast Cancer British Medical Journal, 1:439, 1976;

Constanza, M. Adjuvant Chemotherapy-Eight Years Later Journal of the American Medical Association, 252:2611, 1984;

Greenberg, D. 'Progress' In Cancer Research-Don't Say It Isn't So New England Journal of Medicine, 292:707, 1975;

Cancer Surveillance, Epidemiology and End Results [SEER] Program, Cancer Patient Survival Report #5 Department of Health, Education and Welfare publication #(NIH) 77-992, 1976;

20.

U.S. War on Cancer A Failure, Says Former Scientist Animals Agenda, September, 1985, p.14;

21.

Robbins, John Diet for A New America Stillpoint Publishing, Durham, N.H., 1987;

22.

McGovern, George, (quoted in) The Boston Globe, June 13, 1978;

23.

Upton, Arthur, (statement by) Director of the National Cancer Institute, Status of the Diet, Nutrition and Cancer Program, before the Sub-Committee On Nutrition, October 2, 1972;

24.

Robbins, John Diet for a New America Stillpoint Publishing, Walpole, N.H., 1987, p.250-51;

25.

Gori, G. (as quoted by Peter Chowka) Cancer Research - The $20 Billion Failure Vegetarian Times, December 1981;

26.

Chowka, Peter as above, p.34;

Gori, G. (as quoted by F. Sussman) Vegetarian Alternative, Rodale Press, 1978;

Reddy, B. Nutrition and It's Relationship to Cancer Advances In Cancer Research, 32:237, 1980;

Committee on Diet, Nutrition and Cancer, Assembly of Life Sciences, National Research Council, Diet, Nutrition and Cancer National Academy Press, Washington, D.C., 1982;

Nutrition and Cancer: Cause and Prevention an American Cancer Society Special Report, CA 34:121, 1984;

Section One - Anti-Density Theory

U.S. Senate Report Dietary Goals for the United States, Select Committee on Nutrition and Human Needs United States Senate Government Printing Office, Washington, February, 1977;

Tannenbaum, A. The Genesis and Growth of Tumours, Ill Effects of a High Fat Diet Cancer Research, 2:468, 1942;

Armstrong, B. and Doll, R. Environmental Factors and Cancer Incidence and Mortality in Different Countries International Journal of Cancer, 15:617, 1975;

27.
Hausman, Patricia Jack Spratt's Legacy - The Science and Politics of Fat and Cholesterol Richard Marek Publishers, New York, 1981, p.103-119;

28.
Ibid. p.116;

29.
Hirayama, T. Epidemiology of Breast Cancer with Special Reference to the Role of Diet Preventive Medicine, 7:173, 1978;

Wynder, E. Dietary Fat and Colon Cancer Journal of the National Cancer Institute, 54:7, 1975;

Weisburger, J. Nutrition and Cancer - On the Mechanisms Bearing On Causes of Cancer of the Colon, Breast, Prostate and Stomach Bulletin of the New York Academy of Medicine, 56:673, 1980;

Mann, G. Food Intake and Resistance to Disease Lancet, 1:1238, 1980;

Reddy, B. and Wynder, E. Large Bowel Carcogenesis: Fecal Constituents of Populations with Diverse Incidence of Colon Cancer Journal of the National Cancer Institute, 50:1437, 1973;

Walker, A. Colon Cancer and Diet with Special References to Intakes of Fat and Fiber American Journal of Clinical Nutrition, 34:2054, 1981;

Phillips, R. Role of Lifestyle and Dietary Habits In Risk of Cancer... Cancer Research, 35:3513,

30.
1975;Berg, John Journal of the National Cancer Institute, December, 1973, p.1771;

31.
Hepner, G. Altered Bile Acid Metabolism In Vegetarians American Journal of Digestive Diseases, 20:935, 1975;

Hill, M. The Effect of Some Factors on the Fecal Concentration ... Journal of Pathology, 104:239, 1971;

32.
Bennion, Risk Factors for the Development of Cholethiasis in Man New England Journal of Medicine 299:1221, 1978;

Broitman, S. Polyunsaturated Fats, Cholesterol and Large Bowel Tumorigenesis Cancer, 40:2455, 1977;

33.
Hirayama, T. (paper presented at) Conference of Breast Cancer and Diet, U.S.-Japan Cooperative Cancer Research Program Fred Hutchinson Cancer Center, Seattle, Wa., March 14-15, 1977;

34.
MacDonald, W. Histiological Effect... Canadian Medical Association Journal, 96:1521, 1967;

Wynder, E. Epidemiology of Adenocarcinoma of the Kidney Journal of the

Section One - Anti-Density Theory

National Cancer Institute, 53:1619, 1974;

Sturdevant, R. <u>Increased Evidence of Cholethiasis In Men Ingesting A Serum Cholesterol Lowering Diet</u> New England Journal of Medicine, 288:24, 1973;

Hill, P. <u>Environmental Factors of Breast and Prostatic Cancer</u> Cancer Research, 41:3817, 1981;

Breslow, N. <u>Latent Carcinoma of Prostate at Autopsy in Seven Areas</u> International Journal of Cancer, 20:680, 1977;

35.

Virag, R. <u>Is Impotence An Arterial Disorder?</u> Lancet, 1:181, 1985;

36.

Kapleau, Philip <u>To Cherish All Life</u> Harper & Row, San Francisco, 1981, p.59

37.

McDougall, John <u>The McDougall Plan</u> New Century Publishers, 1983, p.7

38.

Robbins, John <u>Diet for A New America</u> Stillpoint Publishing, Walpole, N.H., 1987, p.149-50

39.

Wendt, L., Wendt, T., Wendt, A., Protein Transport and Protein Storage in Etiology and Pathogenesis of Arteriosclerosis, Emahrungswiss, Dietrich Steinkopff Veriag, 1975 pp.1-38 Research introduced to the U.S. by Viktoras Kulvinskas Wendt as quoted in Spiritual Nutrition and the Rainbow Diet; Cousins, Gabriel M.D., 1986. p.108

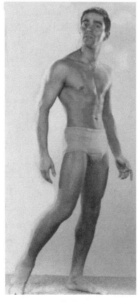

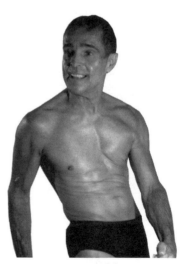

age 64

age 26

David Carmos in January 1967 and February 2006

Section One - Anti-Density Theory

Section One - Anti-Density Theory

Vitality & How To Get It

Eating is universal. No matter where we are on the planet, eating always plays an important role in every culture. If you asked ten different people why they eat, you would always receive the same basic answer, "I eat to live" - in spite of the fact that many people seem to live to eat. Yet, no matter how much food you consumed, or how well balanced you assumed it to be, if you were listless a good deal of the time, one knowledgeable about health would probably suggest that "maybe there is something wrong with your diet".

We in the "enlightened" West are taught that energy comes from calories. We are also taught that just about everything in our Western diet contains calories. Therefore, the general assumption is that the more we eat, the more calories we consume, the more energy we will have. It is also generally assumed, that if one eats a "good variety" of what food is commonly available, then one will have general "good" health.

Times Change

Fifty or sixty years ago, that was relatively true. Unfortunately, with the advent of carcinogenic additives and the extreme refining and treating of most all food stuffs, it is no longer in the range of relativity. Coupling that with the fact that the plethora of prescription and non prescription substances which the average person doses themselves with, that can and often do affect the delicate chemical balance in our bodies, the problem is compounded even more.

Section Two - Vitality

Environmental Effects

Air pollutants affect the absorption of all vitamins. Excessive alcohol consumption affects vitamins A, the entire B complex, D, E, K and magnesium. Carbon monoxide which is spewed out by automobile exhaust destroys vitamin C. Chlorine destroys vitamin E. Caffeine containing substances affect vitamins B1, inositol and biotin, and the minerals calcium, potassium, zinc and iron. Fluoride robs the body of vitamin C.

Nitrates & Nitrites

The nitrates and nitrites which are used in the processing of cold cuts and some " fresh meats" to add color and prevent rancidity of the fat are sodium salts and will tend to raise the blood pressure. To make things worse, the nitrites once in the stomach can combine with the *amines found in protein foods (which are usually the type of foods nitrates and nitrites are added to), and create nitrosamines, which at present are recognized carcinogens. Vitamin C can counteract this, but as is mentioned above, is destroyed by the fluoride in common drinking water. Refined sugar, flour and tobacco robs the body of the entire B complex. Along with these, tobacco also robs the body of vitamin C and the minerals calcium and phosphorus. Stress draws on the body's supply of all vitamins. Menstruation affects the body's supply of B 12, iron, calcium and magnesium.

Effects of Antacids

To compound things even more, the many antacids which people use to settle an unsettled stomach from eating incorrectly, draws on the body's supply of vitamins A and the B complex. Antibiotics affect the B complex and vitamin K, while aspirin draws on the supply of vitamins A, B complex, C, calcium and potassium; and barbiturates (downers) play havoc with vitamins A, C, D and folic acid, another B vitamin.

Common Beliefs

In America, we have grown up accepting over the counter preparations as well as prescription drugs as part and parcel of maintaining health, while in reality, these things are what one might go after when they are not really feeling healthy.

On the other hand, there are natural medicaments which can have a similar effect, often without the deleterious results drugs bring about.

What Is True Health?

The average person is not healthy, they just are not clinically sick. Their vitality is waning by the time they are thirty years old, with the emphasis on old. Their bowels probably have not functioned well in years, their digestion is slow, their breath is bad, they have chronic headaches, they require pills to put them to sleep at night, and stimulants to wake them up in the morning.

Many people are addicted to coffee, tea, cigarettes, aspirin, and the various uppers" and " downers" which we so often consider to be a standard part of civilized life. They just assume "If I need more energy, I'll just eat more calories".

Section Two - Vitality

Calories - Quality vs. Quantity

Casual observation will show that this is not always true, if it were, with about 3500 calories to a pound of fat, the fatter we were, the more energy we would have. A person two-hundred pounds overweight, with about 700,000 excess calories, would have boundless energy. Another, four hundred pounds overweight, would have at least twice as much energy as the first person; but the plump are not the energetic ones as a rule. It is generally the lean who are always going, always "charged up".

What gives one person drive, and the other none at all? First is the quality of the calories taken in. More than that is the ability of the body to utilize the calories taken in. Beyond that, one may have a nutritionally sound diet which does not build health or impart vitality at all. In other words, your diet may comprise a sufficient number of grams of protein, carbohydrate and fat, and an amount of calories considered sufficient for your body structure to function properly, but you may not exhibit any of the signs of health.

You may wake up every morning with a heavily fetid breath, "eye crunch", dandruff, pimples on several areas of your body, occasional backaches, toothaches, headaches, neck aches, stomach aches, chronically constipated, or with occasional diarrhea, falling hair, falling arches, diminished sex drive, impotency, failing eyesight, progressive hearing loss, rotting teeth, and the endless plethora of conditions which the average human being considers to be part and parcel of our progressive day to day human condition.

Nature Offers Us A Seven Year Renewal

When we consider the fact that no one cell in the body is more than a year old, and that every cell in the body will be completely renewed in a seven year period, then we realize that we have the ability to create our own potential in any direction we may want to progress; whether it be health, youth, vitality, Intelligence, knowledge or an understanding of any of the aspects of our life.

The Guna (see p.52)

(see p.52)

Sattva - fresh fruit, vegetables, whole grains, nuts, seeds, dairy, spiritually developed people, love, patience, compassion, tolerance, focused

Rajas -meat, fish, eggs, hot spices, stimulants, alcohol, average person, high blood pressure, restless state of mind, satisfied to get by

Tamas - overripe, putrefied, rotten, aged & smelly foods, dull, spiritually undeveloped, likes conflict & aggression, leans toward negative

Our True Purpose
After considering this, simple logic will lead us to the idea that we were not placed here to gradually rot away in pain, but to progress and to grow in every direction we can. Anything which tends to hinder our growth should be eliminated from our lives. If for some reason we cannot eliminate, then we need to adjust to the hindrance. Even adjustment is a type of hindrance; but better than no adjustment at all.

If we research a little further, we will see that people who fast correctly can also have tremendous energy. Where are their calories coming from? If it is from the release of stored up calories, then where were those calories when the body needed them previously? When you consider the fact that our diet and consequently our caloric storage often contains "empty" calories; which have been refined to the point of containing little nutritional value, would it have mattered if the calories had been released?

Ancient Nutritional Concepts
In ancient times did they balance things nutritionally as we do in more modern times? In ancient times, eating was not based on protein, carbohydrate, fat and calories. Eating was either based on yin-yang values, or people merely ate what was available in the area. People lived, and nations prospered, and developed sciences, philosophies, wise men and healers. Unlike our modern Western society, most ancient people ate relatively little. What they ate grew mainly in
Section Two - Vitality

the climate in which they lived. In ancient times the "enlightened" ones recognized three qualities of life. In the Sanskrit these qualities were known as the *guna* or *prakriti*. (see graph on p.50)

According to the guna, the most highly evolved person lived on the simplest of diet, and in the simplest manner and philosophy. A person highly evolved physically, emotionally and mentally ate little. How did these people survive? They believed mainly in the purification of the inner being. They strived to obtain such a goal. In their striving, they sought to eliminate those things which allowed them to live lackadaisically. They worked on developing discipline in every aspect of their lives.

3 Main Types of Food

There are three main types of food for humans - solid, liquid and gas. Of these, which is the most important? For how long can we go without solid food - ten, twenty, thirty days? Yes! We can survive without water for several days; but for how long can we go without air? Not too long. So it is quite evident which is the most important source of energy for humankind.

Even in our standard way of living, when our level of health is not at the height that it should be, when our systems are clogged, sluggish, slow or non-functioning, air is still the most important element in the human dietary.

When we do eat solid food, what is absorbed into our body comes through the liquid part of the solid food, which is broken down by chewing,

Topside   Underside

P=Physical M=Mental E=Emotional S=Spiritual

enzymes and hormones; and then absorbed into the blood stream to supply what our body might be lacking to function at its optimum. What is passed out of our bodies is waste, residue, excess which cannot be stored, and the solid matter which cannot be absorbed. All of the above elements along with vitamins, minerals and amino acids, must be in correct proportion and proper condition for our systems to work consistently well.

Because the various elements needed by our body systems are synergistic with each other (that is, they work with each other in proportion to what is required), it is important to take in what is needed. If there is a prolonged imbalance, the elemental integrity of our being is thrown off, and often one system will begin to borrow from another.

Section Two - Vitality

7 Forms of Food

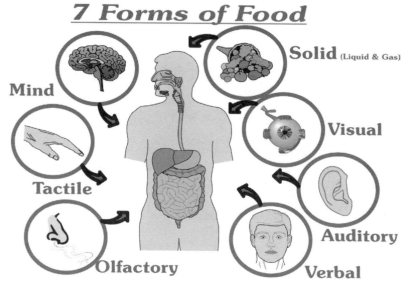

Mind

Solid (Liquid & Gas)

Visual

Tactile

Auditory

Olfactory

Verbal

9 Body Systems

At this point, it might be helpful to explain just what the various body systems are. The systems are.

RESPIRATORY - which involves our lungs, and anything connected with our breathing.

SKELETAL - which involves our bones and some of the hybrid soft/hard tissues.

CIRCULATORY - which involves the movement of the blood throughout the entire body, supplying the organs, muscles and tissues.

REPRODUCTIVE - which involves not only the sexual glands, but also the creation of many of the male/female characteristics which each of us exhibit in our expression and movement as well as in our physical, mental and emotional growth.

ENDOCRINE - involves our glands and the manufacture of hormones which affect us physically, mentally and emotionally.

Section Two - Vitality

EXCRETORY - which involves the elimination of waste from our body, both solid and liquid.

NERVOUS - which is the electrical circuitry receiving, interpreting and delivering the various messages needed to allow us to function in a coordinated manner.

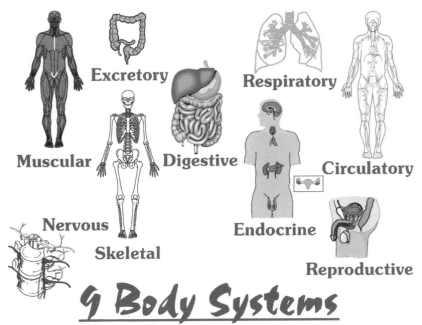

Excretory   Respiratory

Muscular   Digestive   Circulatory

Nervous   Endocrine

Skeletal   Reproductive

9 Body Systems

MUSCULAR - which allows for movement of our body through contraction and relaxation of those fibrous tissues attached to the bones.

DIGESTIVE - The internal organ system which receives, breaks down, changes, absorbs, recreates, distributes and stores the various elements which are taken in constantly and continually.

All of these systems interact with each other with the result that the ***RESPIRATORY*** system not only supplies oxygenized blood for the body, but it also eliminates the carbon dioxide residue picked up by the blood which has just passed through the body.

The **SKELETAL** system not only gives support to the body and allows general body motility, but it also manufactures new red blood cells to help the body function, and new white blood cells to help the body fight infection.

The **CIRCULATORY** system along with carrying the nutritive elements of the blood to the various organs, also picks up waste elements which are important to eliminate from the blood, and supplies warmth to the body tissues.

The **REPRODUCTIVE** system along with creating some glandular secretions which give us our characteristics, also supply us with materials which create lubrication in our body and give us the energy to perform whatever task we may set out to do.

The **ENDOCRINE** system involves the various glands in our body which manufacture hormones which build our tissues, lubricate our joints and organs, create our immunity to foreign invading substances and give us drive.

The **EXCRETORY** system is designed to eliminate all that which the body considers unnecessary whether good or waste. It accomplishes this through the lungs, liver, intestines, kidneys and skin.

The **NERVOUS** system is the catalyst to activate the whole body into action. It works in a very subtle, internal, continual flow, maintaining the balance of the entire body; and in a more external, dynamic manner according to our particular needs at a given moment. The subtle, internal flow does not require any conscious decision on our part, while the external, dynamic one does.

The **MUSCULAR** system along with movement also gives shape and power to our structure, as well as support and massage to the internal organs.

The **DIGESTIVE** system takes a lot of disrespect from our attitude toward ourselves, and helps us to repress those emotional things which we do not want to deal with at the moment.

In other words, it handles and stores for us, all of the "food" sources we take in, whether they are verbal, auditory, tactile, sensory, olfactory, visual or mental, until we reach a saturation point, and then allows us to purge ourselves of them until our buildup drops to a level we can comfortably live with. These various food sources will be dealt with next.

Food - One of Life's Great Tranquilizers

Often we think of food as solid only. It was pointed out earlier that the main types of "food" we take in are solid, liquid and gas. Actually, anything which is received by or through our various senses is "food" for our human organism. Consequently, there is mental food, auditory food, visual food, tactile food, sensory food, and olfactory (aromas) food as well as verbal food.

Any one of these forms of food can relax or excite part, one, some or all of our various body systems. The result can be love or anger, excitement or depression, health or a lack of it, depending on how and when we receive the "food" and the way in which we interpret it.

Why does our physical, mental and emotional energy rise as we fast, and as we evolve from a more dense form of energy to a more etheric source of energy? Because energy in the true sense of the word comes not from calories, but from viscosity of tissue - that is, from the ability of the tissue to rhythmically expand and contract. Children have good viscosity, the aged do not. No matter our chronological age, as soon as we begin to lose flexibility, whether physical, mental or emotional, we have begun to age.

When a child is born, its rear is slapped, this causes a contraction from the buttocks to the abdomen through the lungs, to force the mouth open. In reaction, the atmospheric pressure forces air from a greater concentration (the outside atmosphere) to a lesser concentration (into the lungs) and man lives.

When this process stops, so does the man. By the same token, as our rate of breathing *increases*, so does our energy level. As our rate of breathing *decreases* so does our tension level.

Energy

When energy flows freely through our body organs and muscle tissue, unfettered by emotional tension and physical tautness, there is vitality. Whenever this energy reaches a point of physical tautness, it emanates as tension. At times we activate more energy than we need, and the result is a hyper-energy. Just as energy flow reaching a point of physical tautness will tend to become tension, hyper-energy reaching a point of physical tautness will tend to become hypertension.

Developing Vitality

The first thing necessary to attain vitality is to develop flexibility, and consequently avoid physical tautness. This can be accomplished by a simple meatless diet (because of meats relatively high uric acid content being a hindrance to flexibility), a relaxed mental attitude, and, extremely important, a slow rhythmic stretching of the entire body. Following this pattern, tension will become energy, and hypertension will become hyper-energy. Slow rhythmic breathing will lower this hyper-energy to a comfortable level.

If one is eating a stimulating diet, the energy level will begin to rise again above the level which can be handled comfortably. This rise will tend to occur without notice, and will sometimes manifest itself as short temper, irritable disposition, mental confusion, or as hypoglycemia, if an excess of simple sugar is taken in.

Functional Hypoglycemia

The body will secrete insulin to handle the sugar, but simple sugars are often absorbed so quickly, that the insulin, after it reaches the blood stream several hours later, is left in excess, causing a low blood sugar or hypoglycemia.

Under stress we sometimes activate tremendous levels of energy. Even though this is more than we could generally handle comfortably, during stress situations, it is not only a good energy level, it is a necessary one.

However, after the period of need has passed, this level of energy is still present. If we do not know how to lower it, the physical, mental and emotional tautness, which was created during the stress will show up as hypertension; then the entire body will vibrate, although sometimes only the face and voice will vibrate. If the vibration becomes too great, a fuse will "blow", and the subject will faint.

Fright or Flight

Classic instances of this are seen when a person is frightened. Examples include such instances as a woman whose purse has been grabbed, fighting the attacker off, even though he is half her age and twice her size; or a passerby lifting the end of an automobile, to pull out someone on whom the car had fallen when the jack slipped.

Under ordinary circumstances these people would never have accomplished such feats, but when the power was needed it was there. How and why? Because long slow breaths or quick short breaths activate energy through an adrenal release and the absorption of what is known in the Sanskrit as "prana". The closest equivalent English term for the Sanskrit "prana" is "life essence" or "life force", "spirit" or "energy".

Intrinsic Knowledge

When we are attempting to lift something extremely heavy, even if we know nothing at all about lifting technique, when we might doubt our ability to even budge the weight, let alone lift it, we will automatically inhale and exhale in either long slow breaths or in quick short breaths, and then retain the breath. The inhalation will charge us with energy or "prana" because of the adrenal release, and the breath retention will give control.

As long as we retain the breath we will retain control. When the breath is released, the muscular tissue relaxes and our control is lost.

Systematic Breathing

Now, if lifting great weights can be accomplished haphazardly in emergencies through quick, short breaths, or long slow breaths combined with breath retention, then how much more could be accomplished, if we practiced this breathing rhythm systematically, whenever the need might arise? It could be used during sports, daily work, while under stress, at times of low energy, and most startling of all to heal another.

How can the energy activated to perform muscular feats, be the same as that required to heal? Simply because energy is energy is energy.

3 Types of Imbalance

Dis-eased conditions are basically of three varieties. They are either due to too much energy, for what your physical organism can handle; too little energy, for what you need; or a good level of energy which is imbalanced.

If a bacterial strain might be present, it is due to the fact that our body energy is out of balance to begin with, and bacteria are merely scavengers, who live on waste substances and imbalances. They are present secondarily, and not as the primary cause.

If a person were ill, showing too much energy, massage could help release the energy block; stimulation of acupuncture or acupressure points which activate a particular organ could be applied with needle, hand or water (as in the use of hydrotherapy), to lower the energy if too high, to raise the energy level if it is too low, or to balance it if imbalanced.

However, if a subjects energy were too low, the "healer" could supercharge her/his own body through breathing, and then transfer the energy.

Occasionally I hear from " psychic healers", "Why not just draw energy from the Universal Source?" If the source is truly universal, then why not just let the subject draw it into him or herself? The fact that laying hands on a person can help, shows that there is some energy transference which is not being obtained by the subject on his/her own. It is better to supercharge your own body before attempting to heal someone else.

Energy Exchange

If the average persons energy were say four on a scale of ten when healthy, and when sick dropped to two, and you attempted to heal the person, while your own energy level was at four, the sick person could draw energy from you and feel better, while your energy level dropped below normal, and you began to feel sick, or at least very weak. Yet, if you

Section Two - Vitality

charged your own energy to say six or seven, you could still feel all right after your own level dropped down to four or five again.

Rules for Controlling Energy

Here are a few simple rules for creating and maintaining this high free-flowing energy level:

1) *long slow breaths or quick short breaths will always tend to activate energy;*

2) *retention of the breath will develop control;*

3) *slow exhalations will relax the body tissues;*

4) *avoid meat, alcohol, refined foods, sugar (even natural fruit sugar), chemically treated foods, coffee, pekoe tea, smoking and drugs (uppers or downers). This way your body will develop your own natural level of energy; unhindered by any stimulants.*

5) *Develop and maintain physical, mental and emotional flexibility at all times. This will prevent the energy from becoming tension.*

6) *When developing physical flexibility, never bounce into an exercise, or the flexibility developed will always be forced, and your tension level will be more difficult to release during times of stress.*

7) *Tension tends to originate at the base of the neck and the base of the spine. Energy distribution originates at the medulla at the base of the brain. If tension is held in the neck, as the energy passes from the base of the brain through the cervical (neck) area, the rate of vibration from the neck downward, will be thrown off.*

Tension Release Exercise

Occasionally, when tense, tired or headachey, while sitting or standing, bend the knees slightly, and place the hands on the hips, thumbs forward.

Draw the neck in as in the manner of a turtle, and then draw the chin forward and up, until a slight contraction is found at the base of the rear neck.

Now draw your shoulders upward, as if to touch them to your ears. If this is done correctly, a vibration will overcome the neck, shoulders and head. Hold this vibration for as long as is comfortable. Following are guidelines for energy activation and tension control.

Raise energy through quick, short breathing;

Lower energy through long, slow breathing;

Control energy through steady breathing.

Always release this slowly, releasing with the fingertips and working the release upward through the arms, shoulders and neck.

Raise tension through conditioning exercises;

Lower tension through relaxation exercises;

Control tension by balancing

Section Two - Vitality

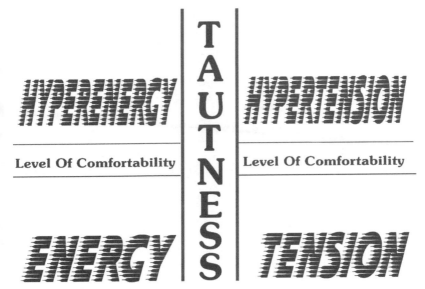

Inhale slightly, retaining the breath during the exercise. The vibration will release built up tension in much the same way that the vibration of hypertension during stress situations will release excess energy.

When the above seven steps(p.63)become part of your daily life, your normal energy state will rise to new levels, and vitality will be yours.

Choosing Food Types

1. When eating, also choose foods which require a good deal of chewing. High fiber foods require more chewing, and the more we have to chew, the less we will tend to eat. These foods will also tend to lean us down. Those foods which tend to keep us slimmer, also tend to impart more vitality to us.

2. Always eat foods in as close to their natural state as possible.

Section Two - Vitality

3. *Learn to restructure your diet. If you are thinking, "I'm going to have to rearrange my whole life in order to eat like this!" you're right. It will simply involve choosing which is more important in your life - living in the dregs with drugs, or learning about Vitality and How To Get It!*

The Breath of Life

Of all the sources of food which we may consume, there is nothing more important than that of the breath. Breathing is the first action that we perform at birth, and it is the last as we depart this earth. It is a source of life more important than solid food or even liquid intake. As important as this is, most people have no concept of how to breathe. The old concept of breathing, using a so-called military breath, by inhaling while drawing the abdomen in, throwing the chest out and pulling the shoulders back, is so opposite to what breathing correctly is all about, that in breathing in such a manner we can only fill about one third of the lungs capacity.

Natural Breathing Patterns

An anatomically correct breathing pattern would involve inhaling diaphragmatically (the diaphragm is a dome shaped muscle in the abdomen), which allows the rib cage to expand (by the pressure of the lungs filling above the diaphragm, to push the diaphragm downward and outward), causing the abdomen to extend slightly. This is the way a baby breathes and it is also the pattern an adult will fall into when sleeping. This is a natural breathing rhythm which allows us to draw in enough air to fully expand

Section Two - Vitality

the lungs. When done properly, the lower part of the lung is filled, middle area and finally the upper part.

Military Breath

As opposed to this is the military breath during the process of which, drawing the abdomen in, throwing the chest out and pulling the shoulders back permits only enough air to enter the chest and fill the upper third of the lung .

The result is that the blood cannot oxygenate sufficiently fast enough, resulting in a continuingly lower energetic level.   Realizing this fact, the yogis created rhythmic breathing patterns to activate, control and disperse the bodily energy. Inhaling will always raise the body's energy. Retention of the breath will give us control, and exhaling of the breath will tend to relax the body. A simple example of this is found when we may attempt to lift something which we might feel is too heavy for us. Automatically, whether we have been trained in lifting technique or not, we will brace our body, inhale in either quick short breaths or in long slow breaths, and while retaining the breath, then lift the object. As long as we hold the breath, we retain the control of our power. As soon as the breath is released the muscle tissue relaxes, and we lose control. Following are some prime examples of these concepts put into practice.

Diaphragmatic Breath

1. Standing, sitting or lying in a comfortable posture with the eyes closed, hand on the abdomen, slowly inhale through the nostrils, allowing the abdomen to protrude in proportion to the inhalation.

Section Two - Vitality

2. Be sure that the shoulders and chest are not raised, since doing so will inhibit deep breathing by drawing the abdomen in and up.

3. If you find difficulty in allowing the abdominal area to drop, attempt the breath lying on the back or in a shoulderstand (lying on your back, hips in the air, vertically above the shoulders. Refer to the section on Rejuvenation). These will facilitate the exercise.

4. When you have inhaled as deeply as possible, retain the breath twice the length of time it took to inhale, and then exhale slowly through pursed lips.

5. Extend the exhalation over a period of time equal to that of the inhalation. Repeat the entire process again and then a third time. Relax at the end of the last round over a period equal to that of the inhalation.

Activating Breath

This may be used instead of the diaphragmatic breath, but never with it, unless under the guidance of a teacher. Together they can cause palpitation and a rise in blood pressure, along with a slight dizziness.

The inhalation is performed with a sharp sniff through the nose and the exhalation is through the mouth with the lips formed in an "O". There is no pause between the inhalation and the exhalation.

This exercise will also clear phlegm from the nasal passages as well as the upper part of the esophagus. Follow this exercise with the diaphragmatic breath to relax the body.

N.B. *Adrenalin, being a hormone of the endocrine system, is secreted directly into the bloodstream, and is present for potential use.*

Section Two - Vitality

Adrenalin is activated by doing this exercise.

In order for the energy which this hormone will bring about to be useful and not create hypertension in the body, always follow this exercise with the diaphragmatic breath or some similar breathing exercise, to slow down the pulsations and bring about greater bodily control.

Cleansing Breath

This is a great activator as well as a good vibrator and ventilator to the lungs.

1. Inhale diaphragmatically, and retain the breath momentarily.

2. Form the lips as if to blow out a candle, being careful not to allow the cheeks to puff.

3. Exhale through the mouth with a snapping of the abdomen, releasing but a small quantity of air.

4. Retain the breath a few more seconds and repeat the exhalation.

5. Continue this action until the capacity of the lungs has been exhausted.

6. Relax.

Since this does activate adrenalin into the bloodstream, do not overdo, and be sure to relax by doing the diaphragmatic breath afterwards.

Kapala Bhathi

This is an activator if ever there was one. The English translation of this Sanscrit term means literally "That which makes the skull shine". It is performed by:

1. First inhaling through the nose and diaphragmatically,

2. Then snorting the air out of the nose, by creating short, sharp contractions with the abdomen.

3. Repeat the inhalation immediately, and continue with the entire exercise.

4. Repeat until comfortably tired.

5. Relax. (Inhalation should be twice that of the retention and exhalation; a 1:2:1 proportion.)

Paul C. Bragg 87, John J. Federkiewicz M.D. 77, David Cooper 69, David Carmos (shortly before his 27th birthday) at "L" Street Beach, South Boston, Massachusetts July, 1968.

Section Two - Vitality

HEALTH

What is Health?

Once we understand what health really is, then we can set out to establish the necessary guidelines to create the level of health which is our ideal. When we begin to examine the facts, we will see that there is no animal in nature which cooks its food before eating it, except for humans and other domesticated animals. In our arrogance we say, that is what separates us from the other species of animals on this planet. True, that fact does separate us, but it does not necessarily make us better, healthier or wiser. Nature is immutable in her knowledge of how to create balance among and within her creatures.

We are programmed from childhood to eat our meals while they are hot. True, that warm food has a certain attraction, and it is also true that the more cooked food one consumes the less desire there is for raw. So the question arises, are there any advantages to eating raw food? The answer is definitely yes!

Enzymes

To begin with, the very life of any food is found in the enzymes. According to Edward Howell M.D., enzymologist, in his landmark book, <u>Pioneering Nutrition</u> enzymes are destroyed at 118 degrees Fahrenheit in moist heat, and can survive up to 218 degrees Fahrenheit in dry heat, such as baking. So the only way to insure you are receiving the enzymes indigenous to the food you are consuming, is to eat it raw, or as close to raw as possible.[36]

Since cooked food can be so addicting, we must gradually wean ourselves from it in order to

Section Three - Health

really appreciate the value of simple raw food. Now when I say raw, that of course does not mean raw animal food. The eating of flesh we will explore in a bit, but let us first look at the possible values of eating non-animal based foods in their most natural condition possible.

America and Canada's 3 Biggest Killers

In the United States and Canada the three biggest killers are heart disease, stroke and cancer, in that order.[37] Statistically, the chance of a man dying of heart disease, while eating the standard Western diet of meat, eggs, and dairy products, in these two countries is greater than 50%. That means if you flipped a coin, with the results being, heads you live tails you die, you would have a better chance of living by flipping a coin, than if you were to eat the standard American fare.

A statistic like that can be pretty frightening. If we cut our intake to lacto-vegetarian, which includes dairy but no flesh, the chances of dying of a heart attack drop to less than 18%. Become a vegan, eliminating all animal products, (milk, cheese, butter and eggs) and the chances of dying of heart disease drop to less than 5%.

Common Factors

Since collectively, heart disease, stroke and cancer total more deaths than all other causes of death in the United States and Canada combined, is there a common factor among these three killer disease states? The answer is a definite yes! That factor is cholesterol. Now, although a human body does require some cholesterol for the manufacture of certain hormones, it needs minimal amounts, which the human structure has the capability of manufacturing itself. The only other source of cholesterol is dietary. The only significant dietary source is the consumption of animal products, as reported in <u>Dietary Goals for the United States</u> prepared by the staff of the Select Committee on Nutrition and Human Needs of the United States Senate, 1977, and other sources.[38]

Heart Disease & Colon Cancer

According to the National Cancer Institute (1973) and the Foreign Agricultural Circular (1976), among six major cities worldwide, San Francisco, Ca., Bristol, England; Santiago, Chile; Ribeirao Preto, Brazil; Mexico City, Mexico; and Guatemala City, Guatemala; the number of deaths from heart disease and colon cancer parallel the amount of meat consumed in these cities per 100,000 population, per kilograms, per year.[39]

Japanese Puberty

According to the <u>Impact of Westernization of the Nutrition of Japan</u>, as reported in <u>Preventative Medicine</u> (1978), Japanese girls are reaching puberty four years younger than their ancestors did due to dietary changes since World War II.[40] Since the end of the Second World War, the Japanese people have adopted a more Western style diet. Studies have shown that the younger a child reaches the age of puberty, the greater the chances of developing certain types of cancer later in life.

Section Three - Health

On September 10, 1976, the Washington Post reported that Dr. Bruce K. Armstrong, of the Perth Medical Centre, Australia, presented to a conference at Cold Spring Laboratory in New York, a report suggesting that diets high in animal fat, might increase the risk of womb cancer. Dr. Armstrong said the principal risk factors included obesity, early onset of puberty, late onset of menopause, a mild case of diabetes and high blood pressure.[41] He also discussed findings that vegetarian women appeared to be at reduced risk, generally experiencing earlier menopause and lower blood pressure.

Westernization and Japanese Nutrition

Impact of Westernization On the Nutrition of Japan-Y. *Kagara, Preventative Medicine*

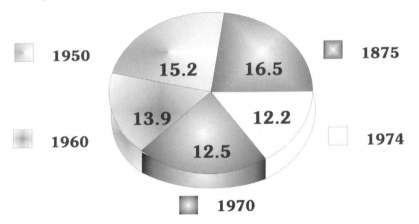

Due to the intake of animal fats after 1945, the age of the first menses began to drop. The younger the menstruation , the more likely the cancer

U.S. Senate Select Committee

The Select Committee on Nutrition of the United States Senate, published its findings in 1977, after more than six years of research into the proposed Dietary Goals for the United States stating

"The Commission recommends that daily intake of saturated fat be less than 10% of total calories".[42]

A major cause of early puberty stems from eating foods of animal origin, with growth hormones in them. This has been a practice since the end of the second World War. Several years ago the practice was banned at a federal level in the United States, but it may be regulated by the individual states.

During the period of 1980-1985, while one of your authors was speaking on a weekly basis in Dallas, Texas, some of the regulars who came to his talks were in the cattle business. One of them told your author that Texas law permitted the use of anabolic steroids, but they could be used only in the ear of the animal, and no less than seventy-two hours before slaughter. On the surface that appears to be a safety measure; but in reality it is a bit of a smoke screen, because (according to my informant), the manufacturer claimed that the substance would be affective for up to 60 to 90 days after use. Further, if placing such substances in the ear of the animal were not effective, they would be placed somewhere else.

Organically Raised Beef

One alternative is to obtain meat that is organically raised and hormone free. The best source for this is at a health food store. The best alternative choice is not to eat animal flesh at all. It is quite practical from a financial standpoint, far healthier for humans, and far less destructive to the ecological balance of our planet.

About six years ago, California had just

completed the sixth year of a drought. The bulk of the water used in California goes for the raising of cattle. The United States Department of Agriculture says that it takes approximately 1500 gallons of water to produce one pound of table ready beef.

Cornell University & the Chinese

Colin Campbell Ph.D., of Cornell University, has headed a study in China, on nutrition in relationship to disease. It is considered to be the most extensive research of its kind ever developed. His studies have shown that the incidence of killer diseases such as we have in the United States, are insignificant among the poorer people of China. Among the more affluent, however, there is a definite rise in heart disease and cancer rates. Although at present, the American Heart Association recommends that no more than 30% of our daily caloric intake be composed of fat, Dr. Campbell suggests that a safer level for our daily fat intake be closer to 15-20 %.[43] For more material on Dr. Campbell, refer to the first section of this book.

What About Protein?

At this point let's look at the inevitable question "Will I get enough protein if I become a vegetarian?" Intrinsically, we are vegetarian by structure. If we examine the

1) formation and arrangement of our teeth;

2) structure and movement of our jaw;

3) length of our alimentary canal;

4) our body's primary method of cooling itself, along with the effects of high levels of the LDL cholesterol deposits, the answer is always the same.

Section Three - Health

Vegetarian by Structure

Out of 32 teeth in a human, there are eight incisors, four above and four below. The function of the incisors is exactly what it sounds like, scissors. These teeth are designed to cut, as in slicing. We cut soft and hard fruits and vegetables, nuts, seeds and grains, in order to break them into smaller pieces and prepare them for further mastication and digestion.

Then we have four canine teeth. These are not true canine teeth. A real canine tooth is a fang. If you want to observe an example, lift up the lip of a cat or dog, and if you are real macho try a lion, tiger or cheetah. These have real canine teeth. Real canine teeth are found only in true carnivores. By design and development a canine tooth is pointed and overlaps with the tooth beneath it or above it. The result is that when these teeth are closed on something, they hook it and then tear or rip it. Human canine teeth have a slight taper and are great for cracking say pistascio nuts, but do not hang down and up overlapping like

Difference In A Vegetarian's Jaw

Vegetarian species on the other hand, chew as does a horse, cow, sheep or human. The third section of teeth, the molars, are flat on top with ridges. Anytime you have such a ridged surface on teeth, and the jaw has the capability of moving vertically and side to side (horizontally), whatever is between those teeth is going to be ground. The things which must be ground in order to be digested properly, are nuts, seeds, hard fruits and vegetables, grains and legumes, after being broken down into smaller pieces.

Section Three - Health

Only a vegetarian jaw can move both vertically and horizontally, because of a ball shaped mandibular hinge. Natural carnivores can move their jaws only vertically. The primary external cooling method for vegetarians is perspiration. Only veggie animals sweat. Carnivores, for their primary cooling method pant, as in the lion, tiger, cat or dog.

fangs. True carnivores do not chew food, they wolf it down, swallowing practically whole chunks.

Human Tooth Structure

8 Incisors=25% (A)
4 Canine=12.5% (B)
20 Molars=62.5% (C)

Incisors - Cut
Canines - Tear
Molars - Grind

INCISORS are for <u>cutting</u> as in hard fruits and vegetables.

CANINES are for <u>ripping</u> and tearing as in flesh. A true canine tooth is a fang.

MOLARS are for <u>grinding</u> nuts, seeds, grains, legumes, hard & soft fruits & vegetables.

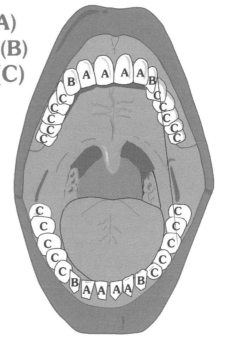

Protein and Fat

The main elements received from the eating of animal products whether flesh or not, are protein and fat. Since a human body cannot absorb straight protein, its need being for amino acids, (which collectively make up protein) the human body must create a protein inversion in order to break down the protein back into amino acids, and then absorb the amino acids. Most vegetable based proteins are already in amino acid form when ingested, so no inversion is necessary. So what about fat?

The National Academy of Sciences, The Select Committee on Nutrition and Health, the American Heart Association and the National Research Council all recommend that our total daily fat intake should not exceed 30% of our caloric intake, with 10% going toward mono-unsaturated fats, 10% toward saturated, and the remaining 10% toward the essential fatty acids (EFAs). Nations with the lowest incidence of fatty degeneration, such as Japan, consume only about 15% of their total caloric intake as fat.

If we compare the amounts of fat found in the most popular animal sources of protein eaten in the United States and Canada, in lean sirloin with the

A Carnivores Stomach Acid

A carnivore has extremely strong stomach acid. Human acid by design is not nearly as strong. Humans on the other hand, must chew food well in order to in salivate and release an enzyme known as ptyalin (tie-a-lin). If this element is not released and mixed into the carbohydrates, (the most efficient form of food energy for humans), while the food is still in the mouth, then further digestion of the carbohydrate foods cannot continue, and a lack of digestion (or indigestion) is the result.

Section Three - Health

fat and pork sausage, 83% of the calories found in these two staples are in the form of fat. Lean T-bone with the fat and lean bacon comprise 82% of their calories as fat. Country sausage is 81%, while spare ribs and frankfurters are 80% fat. Lean ground beef finds 64% of its' calories in fat, and the dark meat of chicken when roasted not fried, is 56% fat, while the light meat of chicken when roasted and without the skin, is still 44% fat in its' caloric content.[44]

Loma Linda University

Loma Linda University, School of Nutrition, because of its Seventh-Day Adventist connection, tends to be more vegetarian oriented in its research, and consequently has researched vegetarian cultures more. It has concluded that the ideal daily intake of fats be no more than 15-20%.

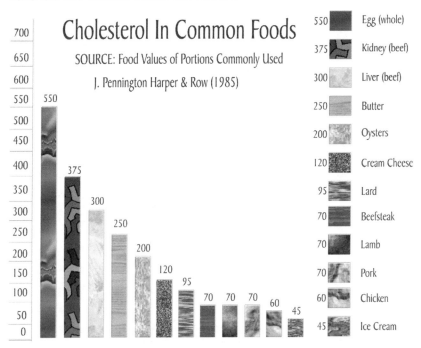

Cholesterol In Common Foods

SOURCE: Food Values of Portions Commonly Used
J. Pennington Harper & Row (1985)

Value	Food
550	Egg (whole)
375	Kidney (beef)
300	Liver (beef)
250	Butter
200	Oysters
120	Cream Cheese
95	Lard
70	Beefsteak
70	Lamb
70	Pork
60	Chicken
45	Ice Cream

Fatty Degeneration

What about those who already have some fatty degeneration (which is probably most Americans and Canadians)? Can anything be done to reverse this condition? The answer is a definite yes! By concentrating on the Omega-3, 6, and 9 factors. These are found in fish oils (salmon, trout, mackerel, and sardines), and also in certain nuts and seeds. It is the EFAs (essential fatty acids), namely, linoleic and linolenic acid. These are imperative to avoid fatty degeneration, and the human body does not seem to have the ability to produce these on its own. Linoleic and linolenic oils are found in walnut oil, and especially in flax seed oil. The catch is that the oil should be organically grown, cold-pressed, refrigerated, kept from light and air, sealed and in an opaque container. It should be used within 6-8 weeks after opening. To be effective 2-3 teaspoons per day should be consumed.[45]

Alimentary Canal

The alimentary canal, (from the mouth to the anus), on an omnivore (designed to consume anything), is 2-3 times the length of its torso. A carnivore's alimentary is canal 3-4 times the length of its torso. An herbivore (vegetarian) has an alimentary canal 6-8 times the length of its torso. A fruitarian has an alimentary canal 10-12 times its' torso.

In the human structure, from the mouth to the base of the esophagus is approximately 18". By definition, the size of the stomach is determined by its contents. The duodenum, the first section of the small intestine, is approximately 10" long. The next section, the jejunum is 14'6" in length; and the ileum, the last section of the small intestine is approximately 7'6" long.

Beyond this is the cecum (or caecum), which is the beginning of the large intestine. This is generally 3-4 inches in length, followed by the ascending, transverse and descending sections of the colon, succeeded by the sigmoid flexure, which leads to the anal canal, and finally the rectum and then the anus. This last area from the cecum on, is four and a half feet in women to five feet long in men.

Humans Are Vegetarian By Structure

X=Alimentary Canal Is X Times the Length of the Torso

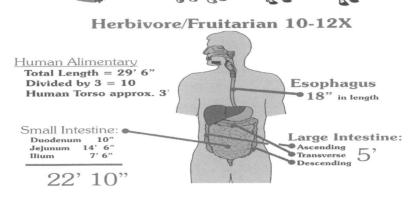

Omnivore

Carnivore
3-4X

Herbivore

2-3X

6-8X

Herbivore/Fruitarian 10-12X

Human Alimentary
Total Length = 29' 6"
Divided by 3 = 10
Human Torso approx. 3'

Esophagus
18" in length

Small Intestine:
Duodenum   10"
Jejunum   14' 6"
Ilium   7' 6"

22' 10"

Large Intestine:
Ascending
Transverse   5'
Descending

When we total the entire length of the alimentary canal, we have 18" (esophagus), plus 10" (duodenum), plus 14' 6" (jejunum), plus 7' 6"

Section Three - Health

(ileum), plus 5' (colon), for a grand total of 29' 4". When this is divided by the length of the average human spine which is approximately 3', we end up with a ratio of 9.8. This places humans in the upper range of vegetarian to the lower range of fruitarian. Many people will claim that we are omnivores. The fact that man has become an omnivore, is a major reason for the majority of his degenerative diseases.

Why Organic?

In the process of growing, plants draw up to 20 minerals plus numerous trace elements from the earth. These need to be replaced. Often organic farmers will rotate crops to allow the earth to replenish. When chemical fertilizers are used instead of the organic, only three to six of the removed minerals are replaced with the result that the nitrogen which is used in large proportions, draws up the moisture from the earth, and creates edematous (water laden) crops, which look good, because they are larger, but are deficient in their essential elements.

Fats & Oils

According to Udo Erasmus Ph.D. in his landmark book Fats and Oils, on page 293 "when cooked food is eaten, a defense reaction occurs in the stomach and digestive tract. This reaction is similar to the reaction we find in infections and around tumors, and involves the accumulation of white blood cells, swelling, and a fever-like increase in the temperature of the stomach and intestinal tissues. We experience tiredness after the meal. The same reaction takes place when half the food eaten is raw, but the cooked part is eaten first. When the raw part of the food is eaten first, however, this reaction does not take place.[46]

Enzymes

The explanation? Raw foods contain living enzymes in their cells which help to digest the food material which we have eaten. This makes it easier for our digestive glands, because they need to secrete fewer enzymes to do the work of digestion."

Flax Seed

Flax has been used since the earliest known periods to maintain healthy animals. Its uses include: correction of digestive disturbances, common in calves, where losses are often very high due to these diseases; feeding of pregnant cows with flax to make birthing easier and to produce healthier calves; to prevent in cattle, infectious diseases such as hoof-and mouth, which often took very heavy tolls, and to make horses' coats glossy. It is also added to the diets of pets to improve their coats, prevent distemper, and improve their general health.

Oil, the fresh oil of the flax seed is the very best oil there is. Fresh flax oil spoils when exposed to light, oxygen and heat, and therefore care needs to be taken in pressing, filling and storing. In North America, formally, this care was not taken, and the oil (called linseed oil) found in health food stores is highly refined and often completely spoiled. The safe shelf life of fresh flax oil, is about 6-8 weeks.

Flax seed oil is the richest of all food sources of linolenic acid, containing between 50 and 60 percent of this fatty acid. It contains between 15 and 25 percent linoleic acid.

Other oils which are high in linoleic acid are safflower, and sunflower oils, but neither of these contains any linoleic acid. Linoleic acid and especially linolenic acid are useful in the treatment of the diseases of fatty degeneration, cardiovascular disease, and especially cancer, although, this research and form of treatment, is carried on only in Mexico and parts of Europe at the present time.

The uniqueness of the flax seed is that it contains a substance which resembles the prostaglandins. The prostaglandins regulate blood pressure and arterial function, and play an important role in calcium and energy metabolism. No other vegetable oil examined so far can match this property of flax oil.

The oil of the flax seed is rich in lecithin and other phosphatides. It contains carotene (pro-vitamin A which has not been found to be toxic in large doses) and vitamin E when unrefined.

Research of Joanna Budwig Ph.D.

Dr. Joanna Budwig of Germany is the worlds foremost authority on the therapeutic use of flax seed oil. She feeds amounts of four ounces per day of fresh flax seed oil to patients with tumors. Her dietary recommendations include plenty of greens, grains, fruits, vegetables. The only animal food she recommends is skimmed milk or cottage cheese, which is combined with the flax oil, and fresh trout because of its omega-3 content.[47]

If any of the essential amino acids is missing

from the diet, then a protein deficiency develops. Flax seed oil has all the essential amino acids and in good balance. It also contains histidine, which although not essential for adults, is for young children. Flax is high in fiber, and fiber prevents bile acids and cholesterol from being reabsorbed through the large intestine. Flax mucilage has the ability to buffer excess acid, decrease the amount of cholesterol being absorbed through food and to stabilize blood glucose. Most all the trace minerals are contained in flax seed, along with vitamins A, B1, B2, C, D and E. It is also helpful as an external compress, and has been used in the Far East since at least third millennium B.C.E.

Hippocrates and Flax

Historically, Hippocrates, in the 5th century B.C.E., mentions use of flax to relieve inflammation of mucous membranes, as well as for relief of abdominal pains and diarrhea. Theophrastus recommends the use of flax mucilage against coughs. Ancient East Indian scriptures state that in order to reach the highest state of contentment and joy, a yogi must eat flax daily. the Roman writer, Tacitus, in the 1st century C.E., passed laws and regulations requiring its consumption. Flax meal has been used for centuries in poultices and compresses and for external and internal ailments. Mahatma Gandhi said: "Wherever flax seed becomes a regular food item among the people, there will be better health."

Basal Membrane

Some years ago in Europe, tests were conducted which demonstrated that the basal membrane also known as the basement membrane, on a baby is thin and porous. The result is that anything a baby consumes, can pass osmotically through this membrane, which lies between the capillary wall and the cell wall. Substances must pass through the basal membrane in order to be absorbed into our system. As we mature, this wall becomes thicker and less porous, so that eventually, the basal membrane actually acts as a buffer.

Osmotic Reaction

Since osmosis allows substances of a greater concentration to pass through a semi-permeable membrane to an area of a lesser concentration, only those substances which are extremely dense, have enough force to work their way through the membrane. Animal based foods tend to have a greater density than non-animal based foods. The density of the basal membrane increases with the increase of animal protein intake. Consequently, when a person shifts to a vegetarian diet, one reason they lose weight, is that the foods they are eating are not concentrated enough to get through the membrane. With time, on a simple dietary regimen, the basal membrane becomes thinner and more porous, allowing simple nutrition to supply the body with its' needs. Many of the worlds top athletes are vegetarian. This certainly is not accidental.

Vegetarianism and Athletics

There is a great number of world class vegetarian athletes. Among them, **Murray Rose**, subject of the book <u>Faith, Love and Seaweed</u>, won

Section Three - Health

three gold medals at the 1956 Olympics, held in Melbourne, Australia. In the 1960 Olympic games in Rome, he became the first man to retain the 400 meter freestyle title. He later broke his own 400 meter and 1500 meter freestyle world records. Another vegetarian Olympic athlete, whose participated sport was Graeco-Roman wrestling, although not nearly as celebrated, is **James Peckham**, an American, who was raised in a vegetarian family.

Edwin Moses, the man Sports Illustrated when awarding him " Sportsman of the Year" in 1984, stated "No athlete in any sport, is so respected by his peers, as Moses is in track and field." Moses dominated the 400 meter hurdles, going eight years without losing a race.

Dave Scott, who is considered one of the greatest triathletes of all time, has won the " Ironman Triathlon" 6 times, including breaking his own world's record three times running. The "Ironman" is the annual event held in Hawaii, which consists of a 2.4 mile ocean swim, a 112 mile bike ride, and then running a full marathon (26.2 miles), all in one event. Dave is an exercise physiologist, who teaches at the University of California.

Sixto Linares, became vegetarian while in his teens. Now in his forties, he competes in benefits for the Special Children's Charity, the Leukemia Society of America, the Muscular Dystrophy Association, the United Way and the American Heart Association. In the summer of 1985, at a benefit for the Muscular Dystrophy Association, Sixto Linares set a record for a

Section Three - Health

one-day triathlon. He completed a swim of 4.8 miles, biked 185 miles, and then run a double marathon (52.4 miles).

Andreas Cahling, the Swedish body builder, who won the 1980 Mr. International Title, is another vegetarian athlete. **Richard Olsen** of Norway, the former Olympic hammer throw master maintained a 4.0 grade average with two majors over a six year period while attending Southern Methodist University in Dallas, Texas during the middle of which time he changed to a vegetarian regimen, under the guidance of one of your authors, to improve his general health and performance.

James and Jonathon de Donato, jointly held the world record for the distance butterfly stroke, and **Alan Jones** a Marine Capt. stationed at Quantico, Virginia, holds the world's record for continuous sit-ups, along with a bevy of other accomplishments including raising a 75 pound barbell above his head 1600 times during a period of 19 hours (September 1974), swimming 500 miles in eleven days through the Snake and Columbia rivers (June 1975), jump roped 43,000 times in a period of five hours (September 1975), jump roped 100,000 times in a period of 23 hours (October 1975), swam 68 miles in a swimming pool without a sleeping break (November 1975), swam one-half mile in freezing (32 degree Fahrenheit) water without a wet suit (December 1975) and completed 51,000 sit-ups in 76 hours (January 1976).

Robert Sweetgall of Newark, Delaware. Is

Section Three - Health

the "ultra long distance runner" in the world. This "moral vegetarian", holds the record for long distance walking and has walked a distance greater than the equatorial circumference of the earth.

Cheryl Marek and **Estelle Gray** hold the World's Record for Cross Country Tandem Cycling.[48] All of the above feats were accomplished by world class performers on a meatless regimen.

References:

40. Howell, Edward, Enzyme Nutrition, Avery Publishing Group, Garden City Park, New York, 1985.

---------Food Enzymes for Health and Longevity, Lotus Light Publications, Wilmot, Wisconsin, 1981.

41. Walford, Roy M.D. Maximum Life Span, W.W. Norton & Company, New York, London, 1983, p. 8.

42. Select Committee On Nutrition and Human Needs, United States Senate, Dietary Goals for the United States, Government Printing Office, February, 1977.

43. Journal of the National Cancer Institute, Vol. 51, #6, Dec. 1973

Foreign Agricultural Circular - Livestock and Meat, USDA, Wash., DC, 1976.

44. Kagara, Y. Impact of Westernization On the Nutrition of Japan: Changes In Physique, Cancer..., Preventative Medicine, 7:205, 1978.

45. Armstrong, Bruce, and Doll, R. Environmental factors and Cancer Incidence and Mortality In Different Countries International Journal of Cancer, 15:617, 1975. pp.158-163.

46. c/f. Ref. 42

47. Campbell, Colin, T., Eat Smart The MacNeil-Lehrer Report, Hosted by Judith Woodruff, MacNeil-Lehrer Productions, 1991.

Robbins, John, Diet for A New America, Stillpoint Publishing, Walpole, New Hampshire, N.H., 1987, p. 201.

48. ibid. p.206.

c/f ref. 41.

49. Erasmus, Udo, <u>The Complete Guide To Fats and Oils In Health and Nutrition</u>, Alive Books, Burnaby, British Columbia, 1986

50. Ibid.

51. Ibid. Budwig, Dr. Joanna, p.272-76.

52. Robbins, John, <u>Diet for A New America:</u> Vegetarianism and Athletes, Stillpoint Publishing, Walpole, N.H., 1987,

Dr. Shawn Miller at age 38

David Carmos age 32 1973 practicing the elbow stand.

Section Three - Health

Of all the appetites which hu-man seems to hold in his possession, the one which satisfies his internal needs, the one for which his craving never seems to cease, the one for which he has developed endless techniques, the one which he has bastardized the most, is his necessity for and consumption of solid and liquid foods. Experience has shown us through our personal encounters, as well as our experience with others over the years, that our human "need" for food is very much dependent on our emotional state at the moment the craving arises. An old dictum in the natural health field is that "Man digs his grave with his tongue".

Reversing the Death Process

In the light of the findings in modern times concerning the effect of various foodstuffs on the human organism, the intuition of that statement seems significant. Yet, the same as humans may pollute their bodies, by eating improperly, we may just as simply cleanse our systems and reverse our swill-bucket state by simplifying our methods of food preparation and consumption. There is an awareness toward and interest in natural, organic and raw food vegetarianism at this point in time, more than at any other period in recorded history. Of the millions of people around the world who are experiencing this reversal of programming, the majority were raised on a standard Western fare.

My Introduction

The father of one of your author's has been a cook since 1927, and a chef since 1929, and as a youngster your author was fed milk and cheese and eggs and meat. On his own at about the age of eleven he began to study what we now refer to as " alternative healing systems". By the age of fourteen he first became vegetarian, breaking it six times in the first six months. However, every time he tried vegetarianism, he felt better than when he wasn't trying it. The problem at that time was that all the available research, was pretty much backed by businesses which were animal based, such as the meat, dairy and poultry industries.

Available 1950s Research

Among the research studies being conducted on the vegetarian lifestyle in the United States, many have been conducted by Loma Linda University, in California. Loma Linda is a Seventh Day Adventist based university. Not all, but many Seventh Day Adventist people are vegetarian by religious belief system, following the guidance in Genesis 1:29. Unfortunately, the book of Genesis does not say "don't cook, or refine or mix foods and chemical preservatives in your stomach", as is done today.

Limited Availability

As a result, companies which produced vegetarian style foods back in the mid-twentieth century, attempted to create synthetic looking "meats". It apparently did not matter whether these foods contained white flour, refined sugar, chemicals (which were not nearly as plentiful as they are today), or preservatives. During the 1950s, the awareness of not eating from a tin can was definitely in the grass roots stage. The availability in variety and quantity of fresh produce was not like it is now, either. Back in the '50s the plethora of fresh fruit and vegetable choices from various cultures and locales around the world was not available to most everyone year 'round, as it is has been for the past twenty years. As a result, your authors experimented with recipes, preparing foods from scratch. We culled these from numerous authors, including those suggested by Jethro Kloss in <u>Back To Eden</u>. Jethro Kloss ran a production company for soy based foods, and was very much into the use of herbs along with several other healing modalities.

Health Pioneers

Many of the early books by pioneers such as Otto Carque, the natural health fields first bio-chemist to concentrate on completely " natural" methods and William Howard Hay M.D. (who was very much into the compatibility of foods.) He included meat, which was the only practical way to go, back in the 1930s. These early books were not available in the 1950s.

Fortunately one of your authors encountered a registered nurse and lab technician, a doctor of medical dentistry, and some medical physicians who were into natural foods. These people were aware of and lived according to natural health methods. They loaned me books which were not easily available, and patiently answered endless lists of questions on health, biochemistry, fasting, elimination, nutrition, and anything else I would present to them, five or six hours a day, day after day, for months. At times I would wear them down, but they would just continue with their work, ignoring me. I didn't want to be rude, but I was so hungry for information on health, and fortunately they understood and cared.

There were other authors, such as Robert Jackson M.D., Howard Inches, Gayelord Hauser, Arnold Ehret, Carleton Fredericks, and the man who stimulated Jack La Lanne, Bob Cummings, Gloria Swanson, Clint Walker and Clint Eastwood's interest in a health oriented lifestyle. That man was Paul C. Bragg. Paul Bragg opened the first "natural food store" in America in 1912. By the time I met him in 1964, when I was in my twenties, I had been a vegan (animal free) vegetarian for eight years.

My Turning Point

Paul started me in lecturing, and due to his influence, I began an adventure with lacto-vegetarianism (includes the use of dairy). After several years as a lacto, I became lacto-ovo (dairy and eggs). In 1965 I first experienced macrobiotics (eating according to yin/yang balance), but back then the guidelines were so strict, I never ventured too far into the system until 1970, when a man I would receive two hour shiatsu treatments from, for a $2.00 donation starting back in 1966, began lecturing on a regular basis on Oriental Medicine. I and several of my friends would be treated by this man three to four times a week, in private sessions. He would allow me to watch during these sessions, and question him as to how and why he did certain things.

This was my introduction to ancient healing techniques using the physical structure as the means

Section Four - Food

of creating balance, outside of yoga which I had been aware of and practicing and teaching since 1952, and teaching at the university level as a therapeutic modality beginning in 1966.

That man is a master when it comes to the concepts of yin/yang. His name is Michio Kushi. He began a newsletter which eventually became the East-West Journal. He later founded a natural foods company in the late '60s, he called Erewhon, and that was the beginning of buying natural and organic foods in bulk containers in the United States. In Macrobiotic circles, Michio is the 'Pope'. He is still speaking, only now world-wide to packed audiences. He is a gentle, quiet man, and a masterful communicator. Michio softened the macrobiotic guidelines from what they had been during the time of his teacher, a man named Nyoti Sakurasawa, more often known in the Western hemisphere as George Ohshawa, the founder and developer of modern day eating according to the balance of yin/yang.

Macrobiotics In the Early Days

Macrobiotics introduced several new foods to the Western health foods market that previously had not been known. Among these foods are tamari, miso, and umeboshi (pickled plum). The Macrobiotic approach has solidified the supply of organic produce and is actually a complete system in itself. Michio's work in treating cancer and certain types of heart disease, has led to research projects at such world renowned facilities as Harvard University and the Beth Israel Hospital in Brookline, Massachusetts, a world famous research center into atherosclerotic disease research and study. The main drawback in macrobiotics has been that in general, there is not a high enough percentage of raw food.

Although Macrobiotics has helped an enormous number of people, in our experience with people on this approach to health, we have found many of them to be chronically constipated, with strong and continual intestinal gas. They are often very irritable, and quite judgmental of others.

On the other hand however, there are many Macrobiotic people who have cleared up chronic colitis along with a host of other chronic conditions. It definitely is leagues beyond the standard American diet of meat, potatoes, excessive amounts of dairy, processed and chemicalized foods, frozen, packaged and prepared foods from which the life force has been removed, the fiber eliminated and what little good was left remaining, adulterated.

Personal Choices

We still eat and live according to the concepts of yin/yang, but are on a very high percentage of living, raw, organic produce. Beans, legumes, grains, seeds and nuts we consume generally in sprouted form. Sprouts are definitely the food of the 21st century. Pound for pound, there is greater nutrition to be discovered in fresh, organic sprouts, than in any other form of food on the planet, and at a cost far more economical than is available from any other source of nutrition for humans. Naturally, these sprouts should be eaten raw. If you must prepare them in some way,

Section Four - Food

apply as little heat as is possible and cook for as short a time period as is possible.

Eating Vibrationally

Everything is vibrational, and that includes food too. According to the particular rate of vibration, things will manifest in a certain manner. This rate of vibration is what determines the color and shape of each specific food. The color scale runs from red (more yang) to orange, yellow, green, blue, indigo and purple (more yin). Orange is the mid-point between red and yellow. Green is the mid-point between yellow and blue. Indigo is the mid-point between azure blue and purple. Purple is between indigo and red. After purple, the cycle repeats itself, beginning with red again, but on a higher octave.

Yin Yang & Food

Laying out our scale from more yang to more yin, we have a pattern of red-orange-yellow-green-blue-indigo-purple. The middle of the spectrum is green. By concentrating on foods of this vibration, and then moving either yin or yang for the remainder of our diet, we can develop a pretty well balanced eating regimen on simple natural foods. Both of your authors are very active, which is more yang, and so we eat foods which are more yin. A person who is less active may eat foods which are more yang, and still create balance to some extent. That is what most macro people tend to do. The drawback is, that it is so nebulous, to create your mental, emotional and physical equilibrium using only food, and attempt to maintain balance by what you eat alone.

Section Four - Food

Climate

The climate one lives in should also be taken into consideration. In a more temperate four season climate, which experiences winters and where the summers range around 65-70 degrees Fahrenheit (18-20 degrees Centigrade), you may eat a little more yang, or may increase your yang activity. We say yang activity because, some activities such as golf and walking really are not active enough. The key to watch for is those forms of exercise which will rhythmically extend and contract all the muscles of the body, in a slow, rythmic manner, and are bi-lateral.

Another Approach

The younger of your authors decided to eliminate candy, cake, soft drinks, ice cream, refined sugars, most processed foods and chocolate at the age of fifteen and even in his late thirties, has never had a cavity. We realize that not everyone has such commitment but each of us can aspire to whichever level you think you are ready for.

Exercise

For a person in average shape, which is really no shape at all, walking and golf seem wonderful. These activities do help to increase the circulation, and create very subtle extension and contraction of the skeletal muscles (those attached to bones), but do not sufficiently exercise either the skeletal or visceral (internal) organs or muscles.

The type of activity which is necessary to create a really superb physical condition is bicycle riding (not always sitting, sometimes posting off the seat),

Section Four - Food

dancing, yoga, tai chi, skiing, weights, aerobics, calisthenics (done slowly), roller skating, ice skating, horseback riding, swimming, basketball, baseball, gymnastics and rowing. Some activities should really be looked at for the purpose of weighing the potential dangers against the possible benefits, avoiding those activities which are one sided or potentially harmful.

Our personal choices at this point in life (and for the past several years), is a combination of aerobics, weights, bike riding and yoga. On a diet of about 90 per cent raw food, with both authors living near the ocean, we both work out five days per week, with a minimum of two, often three and sometimes even all four forms of exercise, spread throughout the day. Now we know that for many people, that is way too much activity, but your choices are going to depend on your goals.

We heard a story several years ago about many people liking oats. Some want top quality oats and are willing to pay the price. Others are more interested in saving money and are willing to wait until after the oats go through the horse. That is the way many people have approached life.

The reasons for our exercise choices are that biking, aerobics, yoga and weights fulfill all of our requirements, while eliminating or at least minimizing any possible detriment. Aerobics and biking provide cardio-vascular work while eliminating the trauma of jogging, weights increase power, and yoga provides stress reduction, power, flexibility, coordination, agility, endurance & energy.

Section Four - Food

Main Reason For Eating

In all the years we have been involved in living a healthy lifestyle, we have never seen such widespread interest among the general public in overall good health from both a nutritional and physical standpoint. When we do have a little cooked food. It is generally a whole grain, a baked yam and/or baked potato. We realize that this is a bit too Spartan for most. It has been our observation over the years with ourselves and literally thousands of others we have guided, that the major reason for eating is emotional. At this writing the authors ages total over 100 years young.

Security Foods

Many people, especially those who are extremely sensitive, eat incessantly of " security foods". These are those things which we were programmed as youngsters to believe were foods which would nurture us. Many people will tell you "I cannot go on a diet. As soon as I stop eating I become like a grizzly bear to be around". For those who think like that, changing their usual eating pattern, is not eating at all. As soon as we eliminate our "security foods", our suppressed emotions begin to surface. Eating seems to be the easiest way to quell the discomfort. Unfortunately, the nurturing foods most people turn toward, are loaded with animal fat, refined flour, refined sugar, and are generally quite concentrated.

At times like this we need to challenge our programming, go beyond what we have been led to believe are the answers to life's dilemmas, and find those things which work in our life. The results of all of

Section Four - Food

the various studies conducted and our own personal experiences of dealing with thousands of people over the years show that ultimately, lifestyle changes are the only way to pull it off successfully.

Transitional Diet

In order to accomplish this as easily as possible, a transitional diet is the best way. Most people cannot comfortably change their way of living cold turkey (excuse us, "cold carrot"). Personally, we believe that we shouldn't even try to. Experience has shown that those who try to change their lifestyle by sheer force of will, always go back to where they were, repeatedly, and then finally give up frustrated. The reason a transitional diet should be followed, is because in order to accomplish a successful lifestyle change, it must not be something you do, but something you strive to become.

In order to achieve this end, we are offering some simple guidelines. When first attempting a change, generally meat is not difficult to drop. What is difficult are the addictions. Salt, alcohol, sugar, and coffee, usually in that order. After dropping meat, generally, there is a tremendous rise in energy and endurance.

After dropping sugar you will usually feel more centered. After dropping table salt, simple foods will begin to taste better, weight begins to drop, blood pressure will usually drop, you become less irritable, and more relaxed. After dropping coffee, you will usually experience withdrawal headaches. Coffee for many is the toughest of the habits to eliminate.

Section Four - Food

Learn To Substitute

To help you overcome the cravings, if we gradually substitute foods which have a similar texture, look, aroma and taste, as the "foods" you are used to, and yet have none or at least very few of the potentially harmful elements, the general good feeling and attitude changes, which will occur, more than compensate, for the patience involved.

Bread

One craving you may experience is for something to chew. As a result, many turn to bread. Most breads are not "good" bread at all. Let us examine bread for a moment. To begin with, if we mix flour and water we end up with paste. If we mix whole wheat flour and water, we will end up with whole wheat paste. Picture flour and water in a warm, damp atmosphere. Picture cooking it 3-4 hours at approximately 100 degrees Fahrenheit. Would the mixture become thinner or thicker? Thicker of course. That is exactly what happens in a human system with pastry and many breads.

The Ancient Essenes

Most people have no concept of making bread without flour. The key is to sprout the grains before making the bread. This is not a new idea. It is mentioned in the Bible in Ezekiel 4:9. Before the time of Jesus, the ancient Essenes, a mainly monastic, aesthetic group who left us the Dead Sea Scrolls, used to make bread without flour, from sprouted grains. Their average life span was upwards of 120 years, during a period of human history when the average life span was 38 years. Most health food stores carry Essene Bread, in the refrigerated section. It is sometimes called Manna Bread.

Ancient Bread Without Flour

The ancient Essenes would bake their loaves in the heat of the desert sun, cooking it from sunrise to noon, then turn it over, and cook it from noon to sunset. If you must eat bread, and most people "must", then this is the bread for you. If you toast it, the grains are dextrinized (the starch is inverted into a simpler form of sugar) which makes the bread taste even better; and it is high in fiber.

What To Spread On Your Bread?

As for what to "spread" on the bread, if you put butter on warm bread, it will melt, so why not just put a little flax or soy or safflower oil, and then a little granulated garlic and dill weed. We are sure you will love the flavor. Many people think that margarine is "healthier" than butter. Even though poly-unsaturated oils are included in the making of margarine, in order to place unsaturated oil into a solid state, it must have some saturation. This is generally accomplished by adding hydrogen, thus the name hydrogenation, but often coconut fat or palm kernel oil is added which are among the most naturally saturated fats in the world.

Flavor Enhancers

In place of table salt there are several alternatives. One which we like a great deal is Vegit, which is a combination of dried herbs. It is low sodium

Section Four - Food

and has no added salt. When we hear that salt is necessary, the reference is to the mineral salts, which are calcium, magnesium, potassium, manganese, sodium, phosphorus, etc. Common table salt is sodium chloride, a manufactured product. The way to receive minerals in their most utilizable form is in the way nature created them to be received; in the form of fresh, live vegetables and fruits, seeds, grains and nuts. The addition of dried herbs, crushed and sprinkled is a very pleasant surprise to the taste buds. Another great addition which is also natural is to crush dried seaweed, such as kelp or dulse, over a salad, or in fact over any meal except a sweet one. It not only adds flavor, but needed trace minerals as well. There are many dry herb combinations which may be used. Bragg Sprinkle is such an herbal combo.

St. John's Bread

In place of milk chocolate, which is cocoa with the addition of milk and sugar, you can substitute carob. Chocolate is another addiction people have, and for the same basic reason as coffee. They both contain caffeine. Carob is also a bean, but does not have caffeine. This is another food of the ancient Essenes. John the Baptist, who is generally conceded by theologians to have been an Essene, ate carob while in the desert. Carob is also known as locust bean or St. Johns Bread. When the Bible speaks of John the Baptist eating locusts and honey, it is referring to the locust bean or carob, and not to the eating of insects.

Section Four - Food

The Essenes would not kill anything and consequently were vegetarians. In fact they were outcast among the general community of Jews. The other sects being the Pharisees and the Sadducees. The reason the Essenes were outcast, was that the standard for paying homage to God during that period of time, was to "sacrifice" an animal, usually a dove, lamb or goat, and burn it as an offering. In lieu of that, the Essenes would take a piece of their sprouted bread, and the juice of grapes (which they saw as the "blood" of the mother earth), and consume that as an offering to God instead. They did this as a matter of history at least two to three centuries before the birth of Jesus. Jesus repeated this at the last supper. This is considered one of the indications that Jesus also was an Essene, along with numerous other signs.

Sprouts - The Fount of Life

The fact is that, the best way to consume any food which can be sprouted, is to do just that. Sprouting may be done anywhere, at home, at work, while traveling, and it can be accomplished in 3-5 days. The variety of seeds which is available, is far more extensive than one would generally imagine. Practically any seed in nature may be sprouted and eaten. Studies have shown that when a seed is sprouted, elements are activated which are not present in the seed in its dry form. Seeds may be sprouted and ready to eat in anywhere from one to six days. They may be grown in one's home, office, or even while traveling.

Section Four - Food

Required Sprouting Equipment

The required equipment is minimal, easy to obtain, simple to use and inexpensive. There is a magic in growing your own fresh, live, organic, produce right in your own window or even in a room without a window. It is quick, and it is easy. Those two factors should be enough to interest the average person; but more than that, it is economical, and the most powerful form of clean nutrition available on the planet today.

Additives To Avoid

In your gradual transition from an animal based regimen, to a simple natural way of eating, you should begin reading label ingredients, if you are not already doing so. To assist you in this matter, We are presenting a glossary of additive definitions, and a list of some of the additives, which it would be best to be aware of. (The list will be found following this section of the book.) We are also including a section on natural additives, the sources from which they are derived, the foods and/or cosmetics they are used in, as well as the benefits from using them.

Seeds

Let's take a look at some of the seeds which are commonly sprouted, and what they contain from a nutritional standpoint.

Aduki - also known as adzuki beans, are small red beans, about the size of a mung bean, both of which are traditional beans of the Orient.

They are also grown in the United States, and were introduced mainly through the macrobiotic

Alfalfa Seeds - are tiny golden colored seeds, about the size of a pin point. This legume is probably the most popular of all the sprouts, and is often used in sandwiches as well as salads. As tiny as it is, it is considered quite powerful, since its roots have been known to burrow 50 to 60 feet into the earth, soaking up lots of nutrients along the way. Alfalfa sprouts are big in the vitamin B complex, along with vitamins A, C, E and K. Among its minerals will be found calcium, magnesium, potassium, iron, selenium and zinc. Although a legume, they may be grown in direct light, which develops their chlorophyll content.

Almond - Of all the nuts, almond seems to be the king. They are a good transitional food, easy to carry with you, and they will last a long time. They are even easier to digest after sprouting for 24 to 48 hours, although don't expect any growth as with most other seeds. They are an excellent source of amino acids, calcium, potassium, phosphorus, magnesium and oil. They contain B vitamins and vitamin E. They may be used to make almond milk, salad dressing, beverages, cereals and desserts. Any seed which has the ability to create a tree is quite concentrated, as opposed to a seed which can create a plant or flower such as the pumpkin seed or sunflower seed; so be aware of this fact and do not overdo almonds.

Fenugreek - is a small golden colored seed, similar in appearance to the alfalfa seed. Fenugreek is a great blood purifier and kidney cleanser, as well as a good source of phosphorus and iron. Some feel that fenugreek has a bite, which we have never noticed,

Section Four - Food

and we do not like hot, spicy flavors. If you find this so, eating or growing fenugreek in combination with other seeds will tend to blend and mellow the flavor.

Lentils - are circular, flat legumes, which go nicely in combination with other sprouts. Their flavor is mild, and they are an excellent source of amino acids, vitamin C and iron. Use only green lentils for sprouting, the red are hulled after harvest and usually will not sprout.

Mung - beans which are probably the most used sprout outside of the health food market, are when fully developed, long and always found in Chinese style foods at restaurants. They are a good source of amino acids, especially methionine, which tends to relax the body. They also have good amounts of vitamin C, iron and potassium. They are great in soups, sandwiches, salads, and loaves. In some areas mung bean sprouts are referred to as soy sprouts, although we have no idea why.

Peas - green and yellow are the varieties available. Whole peas must be used for sprouting, and when split, the peas may be used for a hearty soup. They are a good source of amino acids, carbohydrates, fiber, vitamin A, iron, potassium and magnesium. Used in salads, soups, dips, loaves and dressings.

Pumpkin Seed - is a larger seed, which is medium to dark green in color. They are great when sprouted, but don't expect long tails as with many other sprouts. Best to soak them for 24 hours before eating, to activate their true goodness. When buying them, take a whiff to insure they have not gone rancid. Rancidity

Section Four - Food

is not only not good to taste, but will release free-radicals. Free radicals are elements which can activate cancers. Seeds are high in amino acids, oil, vitamin E, phosphorus, iron and zinc. Pumpkin seeds are used in salads, dressings, desserts, beverages and snacks.

Rye - is a grain which looks like a wheat berry, but is grey in color and high in amino acids, B vitamins, vitamin E, phosphorus, potassium and magnesium, when sprouted. They are great when mixed with other grains, and lend themselves nicely to breads, salads and granolas. Rye goes well with barley.

Sesame Seeds - come in light and dark varieties. They are sold hulled or unhulled. Buy unhulled for sprouting. They are rich in amino acids, oil, B vitamins, vitamin E, magnesium, iron, potassium, phosphorus, calcium and fiber. Because of their size, sesame seeds sprout quite quickly, usually in 1 to 3 days. They make great milk, and are good in dressings, bread, cereals and desserts. The darker variety has a stronger flavor.

Sunflower Seeds - are great for traveling, since they are easy to transport and are loaded with nutrition. Being a storehouse of amino acids, oil, B vitamins and vitamin E, they are among the most desirable of seeds. They are packed with calcium, iron, phosphorus, potassium and magnesium; are great in dressings, make a dynamite milk, and are a flavorful addition to breads, desserts and candies, greens are excellent in salads. Any flower which has the intelligence to follow the sun as it moves, the way the sunflower does, has to be special.

Section Four - Food

Wheat - the most used of the grains worldwide, which unfortunately has caused a little problem with some people because they have overused it, and often get reactions to it. Because of this we have suggested in several of the recipes which follow that brown rice flour be used instead of whole wheat. Sprouted wheat is an excellent source of amino acids, carbohydrates, magnesium, phosphorus, and vitamins B and E. It works well in salads, desserts, breads and cereals. For sprouting, buy the soft spring wheat, rather than the hard winter wheat, or use tritacale.

Vegetable Seeds - such as cabbage, kale, mustard, radish and watercress, sprout well, and if planted in 3 to 4 inches of soil make great greens. Vegetable seeds tend to have more of a bite than legumes or grains, which is an indication of their cleansing ability.

Preparing To Sprout

A few guidelines:

1. Always keep growing sprouts moist.
2. Always provide adequate drainage.
3. Always provide adequate air circulation.
4. Keep sprouts out of the sun while growing.
5. Use wide-mouthed jars.
6. Always cover jars with cheese-cloth or nylon mesh screening, or some other non-toxic screening.
7. Secure screens with a rubber band.
8. Never overload jars. (Smaller seeds should just cover the bottom of jar. Larger seeds should not rise more than ¼ inch to ½ inch up the jar.)
9. Always use clean sprouting jars.

Section Four - Food

How To Sprout
Measure the appropriate amount of seed into the jar. Cover the jar mouth with screening. Fill the jar halfway with water. Allow the seeds to soak for the required time. Usually 4-6 hours for the smaller seeds and 12 hours for the larger seeds and beans (refer to sprouting chart). After the incubation period is up, drain off the water, placing the jar mouth down, at a 45 degree angle. For best results the sprouts should be rinsed 2-3 times a day. If foam is seen when rinsing, that is to be expected. When the sprouts have matured, rinse them lightly, and then place them loosely in a large zip lock bag or a jar with a solid cover. New sprouts will keep 7-10 days if kept in a cold atmosphere (refrigerated).

Sprout Bags
Sprouting bags are great for traveling, camping and pretty much eliminate excuses for not having good food when you travel. The most common size is 8 X 12 inches; which is the approximate equivalent of a half gallon jar. They are quite easy to use. You simply place the required amount of seed in the bag and soak it in water for the necessary period of time, hang it to drain and then place the sprouting bag in a larger plastic bag with a few holes cut to allow for ventilation, and hang again. Rinse the seeds twice a day. Simply pull the sprouting bag out of the plastic bag, rinse, drain and replace the sprouting bag in the plastic one again.

Sprouting Chart Guidelines

Variety	Soak/Hours	Amount	Harvest Size	Ready/Days	Size
Aduki	12 hours	1 cup	½" to 1"	3-5 days	
Alfalfa	4-6 hours	3-4 tbs.	1" to 2"	4 to 6 days	
Buckwheat	12 hours	½ cup	5" - 8"	7 days (Lettuce)	
Garbanzo	12 hours	1 cup	½ inch	2-3 days	
Green Peas	12 hours	1 cup	½ inch	2-3 days	
Lentils	12 hours	1 cup	¼" to ½"	3-5 days	
Mung	12 hours	½ cup	½" to 2"	3-6 days	
Kidney	12 hours	1 cup	¼" to ½"	3-5 days	
Radish	4-6 hours	¼ cup	1 inch	4-5 days	
Sunflower	8 hours	2 cups	up to ½"	1-3 days	

When starting a new batch of seeds, always wash out the sprouting bag with soap and warm water. Rinse in cold water several times.

Growing On Trays

A third approach to growing sprouts is the tray method. Kits are available at health food stores in which several trays may be stacked, one on top of the other, allowing diverse kinds of seeds to be sprouted all at the same time, and allowing seeds which do not require light such as legumes and grains to be grown on the lower level shelves. It is as simple as laying the seeds on the tray and setting the trays in a pan of water for the required time, or if you like, start the seeds in a jar for 2-3 days and then transfer them to the trays after a little growth has occurred. This is even more important if the unsprouted seeds are too small for the tray holes.

One other approach for trays with holes larger than the seeds being used, is to lay a sheet of nylon mesh across the bottom and sides of the tray and then lay the seeds down. Mung and aduki beans grow best away from light and under slight pressure.

Harvesting

When ready to harvest the sprouts, place them in a large container. Fill it half way with water, and gently stir the sprouts to loosen any hulls. These will rise to the top. Skim by utensil or hand.

Do your best to get into the habit of eating sprouts as often as possible. The changes which will occur almost instantaneously with your health, energy, outlook, skin clarity and tone, vitality and elimination, will be greater and more startling than you can possibly imagine.

Biogenic Foods

Biogenic means alive and capable of transferring life force into a human or animal body. All raw, unsprouted seeds, grains, beans and nuts are *biogenic*. Fresh raw fruits and vegetables are *bio-active*, that is, while high in life-giving elements they do not have the ability to beget life. When you eat a sprout, you are receiving nutrition at its highest form from a tiny, easy to digest plant at the peak of its nutritional value. When you eat a sprout you receive the best of what the seed has to offer.

In the 16th century Pen T'sao Kang Mu compiled by Li Shih Chen on pharmaceuticals and herbs, which took close to thirty years to complete, recommends sprouts to build and tone the body and to reduce inflammation. Edmond Bordeaux Szekeley, a researcher into the ways of the ancient Essenes, and formulator of the word " biogenic" said, "Germinated and sprouted seeds are instinctive, primeval foods of man, with many millions of years of phylogenetic (evolutionary) affinity."

Hunzas Ancient Novagenerians

The Hunzas, an ancient civilization, who when rediscovered in the early 20th century, living in the mountains near Tibet, were fathering children with the men in their 90s, and their women were becoming mothers, as late as in their sixties. John Tobe in Healthy Hunzas states that "the Hunzas rely on sprouts", which they eat during the winter months and before the spring crops which in themselves are meager. Captain Cook in the 18th century, tested the anti-scurvy properties of sprouts. He found that sprouts were quite effective in eradicating scurvy. The symptoms of scurvy are a lowered risk to infection, bleeding gums, painful, swollen joints, weakness, bleeding under the skin and loose teeth.

Anti-Scurvy Citrus

Captain Cooks use of sprouts continued until the effectiveness of citrus fruits in preventing and treating scurvy was discovered. John Wiltshire, a British physician tested scurvy patients with both lemons and sprouts, using sixty patients in two groups. One group was given four ounces a day of lemon juice, the other group was given four ounces a day of haricot sprouts. After a month of treatment, those on sprouts showed a greater improvement than those on the lemon juice.

In 1938 in India, there was widespread scurvy due to crop failures. In 1940 a program was created that, it was hoped, would eliminate the problem entirely. The initial program was comprised of over 200,000 people. Each was given an ounce of chick peas (garbanzo) or dried sprouted grain once a week. After sixteen weeks of this treatment, the scurvy had been eradicated. In the fall of 1940, scurvy took over a thousand more lives than the previous year. In January of 1941 the sprout program was reinstated, this time to 140,000. After sixteen weeks the scurvy was again eliminated.

During World War II, Dr. Clive McCay of the

Cornell University School of Nutrition, developed a similar program in anticipation of protein shortages in the United States. This was a combination of sprouted grains, beans and seeds. The United States Government Printing Office even published books on the subject, but the expected shortages never occurred, so the program was never implemented. The fact that governments have explore the great potential of sprouts in time of potential famine is indicative of the power of sprouts to deliver power packed nutrition quickly, and at economical prices.

Supplements

When buying vitamins always choose those without artificial colors, artificial flavors and/or preservatives. These are all ingredients commonly used in commercial vitamins. Actually, there are only a select few manufacturers of vitamin and mineral raw materials. All companies that are tableters and manufacturers of vitamin and mineral supplements, use basically the same ingredients.

The main difference between the various brands are the additional ingredients which are used. These involve sugar, preservatives and coloring agents. The other differences lie in which elements are used in making the tablet or capsule. Essentially, vitamins, minerals and other supplements in tablet form are manufactured products. A supplement may be a single element or may be a combination of several elements, such as multi mineral combinations, or amino acid/mineral combinations.

Be Aware of Terminology

There are certain terms you might encounter when reading a vitamin or mineral label. It is important that you understand what is on the label. A rule we have followed for years is, "If you come across a term that you cannot pronounce, don't eat it!" The original concept was created to avoid ingesting chemical substances. In recent times however, there have surfaced elements which have been named by other cultures. These may be difficult to pronounce if you are unfamiliar with the original language.

From a purely chemical standpoint synthetic elements are generally no different from the natural. Yet, what about those elements which are an integral part of the compound, but which have not yet been defined or even discovered? Another concept we encounter is that the sugar found in a banana is no different than that found in a soft drink. From a chemical standpoint this may be true, but we think of it more as observing a set of twins lying down. One is sleeping and one is dead. On the surface they appear identical, yet one has the ability to create life and the other does not. Along with this, is the fact that depending on the stage of ripeness in the banana, the sugar may be more complex than the simple sugar found in a soft drink. There is also the element of ingesting empty calories in the soft drink. These are calories that contain no nutritional value. There are several excipients commonly used to create various effects in vitamin and mineral preparations. The most common we will explore here:

Section Four - Food

Excipients

binders - are substances that give mucilaginous qualities to powdered materials. Among the most common is cellulose.

chelation - (key-la-shun) is the process by which minerals are bonded to amino acids, since the body has an attraction for amino acids which are the building blocks of protein. The amino acids may be from animal or vegetarian sources. The vegetable sources are generally soy and/or rice proteins.

disintegrants - these elements are added to the compound to help the highly compressed tablets dissolve once entering the stomach in order to release the active ingredients. Among the most common are cellulose derivatives which expand when wet.

excipients - are made from a variety of elements and used to impart texture, consistency or form in making tablets. In making tablets, excipients must be used. Among the most common excipients are binders, disintegrants, lubricants and fillers.

fillers - the purpose of fillers is to increase the bulk of the compound, in order to match a particular mold out of which the tablet will be formed. This is done through compression of the ingredients. Common fillers are cellulose and various forms of calcium.

gelatin - most gelatin is animal based and composed of animal parts which are unusable in any other industry. These parts include lips, snout, and anus in sterilized form, and although composed of protein they may not contain all the necessary amino acids. Some gelatin is manufactured from vegetable sources, such as fruit pectin or agar-agar from seaweed.

lubricants - are inert elements added in minute amounts to help expectorate the finished product from the mold. Most common are vegetable based stearates i.e. magnesium stearate and stearic acid.

synergistic - such substances work with other more important elements and assist these elements to increase their efficacy. Common synergists are the bioflavonoids used in conjunction with vitamin C, rosehips, and even vitamin C itself.

Vitamins & Minerals

Following each explanation is the RDI or the *Reference Daily Intake*. Previously the listed amount was called the RDA also known as the *Recommended Daily Allowance*. In reality this was really the MRDA or *Minimum Recommended Daily Allowance*. These were exactly what they said they were, namely, recommended daily minimums. Most people assumed that this was a healthy dose, when in reality it was what the government suggested as the minimum an adult should receive per day. One example of this was with vitamin E. The recommended daily allowance was 30 IU, which is an amount far below the 400IU daily intake that research has found to be necessary in order to be efficacious.

Next is a general outline of the main vitamins and minerals, including their purpose and function:

Vitamin A - This is a fat soluble vitamin necessary for new cell growth, to maintain healthy skin, hair, and mucous membranes. Aids in cell differentiation and visual acuity at night. This vitamin is stored by the body and can be toxic in large amounts, accumulated over an extended period of time. Beta carotene is not a vitamin, but acts as a precursor which the body converts into vitamin A. Unlike Vitamin A, beta carotene is not toxic in high doses. Beta carotene is also known as pro-vitamin A, and is a valuable anti-oxidant. Vitamin A is found in yellow and orange fruits and vegetables, including carrots, sweet potatoes, yams, pumpkin, winter squash, asparagus, kale, brussel sprouts, cherries, watermelon, cantaloupe, mango, apricots and peaches.

Vitamin B$_1$ - (Thiamine) Necessary for the enzymatic conversion of carbohydrates and fats into energy, to support the nervous system, increase the learning capacity, to treat fatigue, depression, irritability, prevent air and sea sickness, to promote healing after surgery, treat alcoholism and Bell's palsy (one-sided paralysis of the face). Addition of thiamine to the diet eliminated beri-beri, caused by eating refined grain products. The best sources are wheat germ and bran, rice polishings, the outer hulls of other whole grains, brown rice, oats, millet, spinach, cauliflower, sunflower seeds, peanuts, peas and beans.

Vitamin B$_2$- (Riboflavin) Used as a building block of co-enzyme A, which the human system manufactures to release energy from foods. Riboflavin is instrumental in maintaining healthy hair, skin, nails, and is necessary for normal cell growth and good vision. It is also used in stress, fatigue, vitality and growth problems. Riboflavin is used to treat acne, eczema, dermatitis, skin ulcers and digestive difficulties. It has been found to be helpful in treating cellular oxygenation, cataracts and leg cramps.

Brewer's yeast is the most abundant source of riboflavin, but brewer's yeast often causes flatulence and bloating in many subjects. Other natural sources are nori seaweed, millet, wild rice, peas, beans, dark leafy greens, broccoli, asparagus, collard greens, whole grains, mushrooms & sunflower seeds.

Vitamin B_3 - (Niacin) Co-functions with enzymes to produce energy from foods. In larger doses it can lower serum cholesterol, act as a blood purifier and also regulate blood pressure. When a sufficient amount of niacin is maintained in the body, the need for protein is lessened. A lack of niacin was the cause of pellagra, the symptoms of which are diarrhea, dementia and dermatitis, mainly from eating refined grains especially refined corn.

Niacin in sufficient amounts anywhere from 50mg. on up, can cause a dilation of the blood vessels, drawing the blood to the surface, turning the skin bright red. Wherever you itch while in this state, is an indication of toxinous residues in the tissue. If you begin scratching, it may feel wonderful, but you will never stop scratching until the niacin wears off. To stop the red flush, simply drink water. The best natural sources are dried beans, peas, wheat germ, whole grains, dates, figs, prunes and peanuts.

Vitamin B_5 - (Pantothenic Acid) Used as a building block of co-enzyme A, which the human system manufactures to release energy from foods. Pantothenic acid is known as the anti-stress vitamin, and is also thought to slow down the aging process and to prevent wrinkles. Pantothenic acid is used to give a healthy sheen to the hair and to help prevent premature graying. After surgery vitamin B5 is used to stimulate gastro-intestinal peristalsis (intestinal rhythm). It is widely found in foods, but is greatly deficient in refined foods. When preparing foods in water, be sure to utilize the remaining water, since B vitamins being water soluble, are leached into the water. Whole grains, peanuts, dried beans, sweet potatoes, green peas and cauliflower are good sources. It is also manufactured in the human intestinal tract.

Vitamin B$_6$ - (Pyridoxine) Promotes proper protein and fat metabolism, participates in neurotransmitter formation, and affects hormone distribution and water balance in women. Pyridoxine aids in fluid balance regulation, and the electrical functioning of the nerves, heart and musculo-skeletal system. With the increase of estrogen levels, more vitamin B$_6$ is required. It is lost in the refining and processing of foods that contain it, and is not replaced in enriched flour. The best natural sources are whole wheat, wheat germ, beans, peanuts and walnuts.

Vitamin B$_{12}$ - (cobalamin)Necessary for healthy red blood cell formation, cell division and nervous system function. Unlike the other B vitamins which are required by the body in milligrams (mg.), ***vitamin B$_{12}$*** is measured in only micrograms (mcg.), since minute amounts are all that is needed, although larger doses up to 1mg. are used therapeutically. Vitamin B$_{12}$ can be manufactured in the intestinal tract, but this function works best when the system is healthy. Until you reach that point it might be wise to supplement your B_{12} intake. Laxatives and the use of antacids tend to deplete the body of its' store of this B vitamin.

Vitamin B_{15} - (Pangamic Acid) has been shown by Russian researchers to reduce the buildup of lactic acid in the body and therefore reduce muscle fatigue and increase endurance in athletes. Other Russian research has found pangamic acid to be affective in alcohol and drug addiction, aging and senility. It is an antioxidant and also helps to lengthen cell life by protecting it from oxidation. It was first isolated from apricot kernels along with laetrile also known as B_{17}.

Beta Carotene - precursor which converts into vitamin A in the body. Fat soluble, anti-oxidant. This helps protect against oxidative cell damage. This is found in yellow and orange colored fruits and vegetables, along with the green leafy vegetables. Beta-carotene helps in growth and tissue healing, serves as an anti-oxidant, stimulates healthy skin growth, and was recently discovered to stimulate T-helper cell activity. (refer to Vitamin A)

Biotin - a B vitamin essential for fat synthesis and the breakdown of protein and carbohydrates for energy. Biotin also helps incorporate amino acids into protein, to help metabolize fat utilization in weight reduction programs, reduce blood sugar in diabetic patients, and slow the progression of graying hair. Avidin the protein found in raw eggs will destroy biotin, and so body builders who consume raw eggs, need to avoid that practice, since it can also lead to fatigue,

Section Four - Food

loss of appetite, depression and nausea. It is difficult to obtain sufficient biotin from food sources, but the friendly bacteria in the intestinal tract manufacture it for us. It is also found in brown rice and nuts.

Vitamin C - is a water soluble anti-oxidant, that promotes iron absorption from plant sources, and is necessary for collagen formation. Vitamin C is widely used in the treatment of the common cold and the flu. It produces a positive immunological response. It helps the body handle stress and fight infections, helps in the formation and maintaining of healthy collagen and brings more rapid healing to injured or aging tissues. The best sources are citrus fruits especially oranges, lemons, limes, tangerines and grapefruit.

Calcium - is the most abundant mineral in the human body, and being such an integral part of so many functions, makes it the most important mineral in the human structure. It works best when in proper proportion to phosphorus at a ratio of about 2 ½ to 1. Calcium helps to keep the blood alkaline, the nerves calm and the muscles relaxed. A shortage of calcium can lead to lower leg cramps. It is also a strengthening component in developing strong bones and teeth, and is integral to the clotting of blood, as well as muscle and nerve functioning. Although advertising and marketing would have us believe that milk and other dairy products are the best sources, in reality dark greens have twice the amount of calcium as dairy products. Recent research has shown that the large amounts of protein in dairy products, causes the kidneys to require an alkaline rinse after flushing out the acid residue from eating animal based proteins. Since calcium is alkaline and abundant, this is pulled from the blood. Since the blood needs the calcium, it pulls it from the bones. This is now believed by some researchers to be a major cause for osteoporosis.

The best sources for calcium are dark greens, almonds, sunflower seeds, pinto, aduki and soybeans, Brazil nuts and hazelnuts. Avoid high oxalic acid foods such as beet tops, beet, spinach and chard as good sources of calcium, since the oxalic acid can form a bond with the calcium and create oxalates or stones, making the calcium not utilizable.

Choline - is a member of the B complex and contains lipotropic or fat metabolizing properties. It is an important part of the neuro-transmitter acetylcholine and is therefore known as the memory mineral. It helps to maintain a well functioning nervous system, is an aid to liver and gall bladder function, muscle twitching and heart palpitations. Other possible uses are as an aid in treating insomnia, headache, dizziness, constipation, tinnitis (ringing in the ears) and hypoglycemia or low blood sugar. Although the human body can synthesize it from the amino acid glycine, the most abundant source is from soybeans, wheat germ, peanuts and some leafy greens.

Chromium - is an essential mineral that works in conjunction with insulin to maintain normal blood/ sugar metabolism. Consequently chromium is used in the treatment of both diabetes mellitus and hypoglycemia. It has been used in conjunction with niacin, the glucose tolerance factor, and in treatment of

Section Four - Food

high blood cholesterol. This mineral is found in whole grains, especially wheat and rye, chili's, potatoes, green peppers, apples, bananas and spinach.

Copper - An important element in enzymes that maintain the integrity of bone, lung cells and blood vessels, and it helps to metabolize iron. Copper aids in the formation of hemoglobin, the oxygen carrying molecule in the blood. Good sources are whole grains, peas, beans especially soy, nuts especially almonds, Brazil nuts, walnuts and hazelnuts. Other sources include green leafy vegetables and some dried fruits; in particular prunes.

Vitamin D - (Calciferol) is known as the sunshine vitamin since sunlight on the skin actually forms vitamin D in the skin. This vitamin being fat soluble can be stored by the body and is therefore potentially toxic in large amounts. Vitamin D helps to regulate calcium metabolism, bone formation, prevents rickets, tooth decay and gum problems, and aids in the absorption of phosphorus. Calciferol also regulates the absorption and use of calcium and phosphorus, which work synergistically, leading to proper muscle and bone function. The best source for a pure vegetarian is the sun, but be careful not to overdo it. (400-1000 IU daily)

Vitamin E - Fat soluble anti-oxidant which protects cell membranes from damage due to oxidation. Research has also connected vitamin E with increased endurance and heart function. Vitamin E comes in two forms, natural and synthetic. The natural form is made from vegetable sources, generally soy, but may

Section Four - Food

also be made from the germ containing oils from oat, wheat or rice. Natural vitamin E in its' chemical structure has the polarity of its' valence, facing to the right. One term in Latin for "right" is "dextro", so the natural form of vitamin E is referred to as "d-alpha".

The synthetic but biologically active form of vitamin E, is generally made from mineral oil. Chemists cannot control the polarity of the valence. As a result, the polarity goes to both the left and the right. One term for "left" in Latin is "laevo". The chemical designation for this is "l", so the synthetic vitamin E is called "d-l alpha". Whenever possible always obtain the "d-alpha" form of vitamin E. The best research says that a minimum of 400IU per day is necessary in order to receive a sufficient amount to be therapeutically beneficial, as opposed to the 30IU minimum recommended by the U.S. government.

Folic Acid - Another of the B vitamins, and named after the Latin folium, because it is found in green leafy vegetables, including kale, beet tops, beets, spinach, chard, broccoli and asparagus. Necessary for DNA synthesis and red blood cell formation. This also protects against certain birth defects.

Inositol - is a part of the B complex, acts as a lipotropic agent, helping to emulsify fats. Some conditions associated with deficiency are eczema, eye problems and hair loss. The best sources are citrus fruits (except for lemons), whole grains, cantaloupe, wheat germ, lima beans, cabbage and soy lecithin.

Iodine - Principal component of thyroid gland hormones, which control body metabolism. When

Section Four - Food

iodine levels are low, goiter or enlargement of the thyroid gland, will develop. The thyroid hormones particularly thyroxin which is 65% iodine, are responsible for our basal metabolic rate (BMR) which is our body's use of energy. These hormones are also needed for normal growth and development, energy metabolism and protein synthesis. Sea vegetables (seaweeds) especially kelp are excellent sources.

Iron - is needed for oxygen transport in muscle and blood, and is one of the elements necessary for producing energy. Along with calcium and zinc, iron is one of the most deficient elements in the common diet. Standard teaching is that iron is difficult if not impossible to absorb on a vegetarian diet. Yet one of your authors while in college in the '60s was in a study for absorption of a hematinic or iron supplement .

Of the twenty students involved in the program, this author was the only vegetarian in the study, and had the highest level of iron of anyone in the test; at the beginning, throughout the testing period and at the end. Signs of deficiency are weakness, fatigue and loss of stamina. The sources of iron he used were beets, beet tops and organic Concord grape juice.

Other natural sources are kelp, sesame seeds, whole grains, wheat germ, millet, oats, brown rice, lima beans, kidney beans, soy beans & green peas.

Magnesium - Catalyst which activates more than 300 enzymes. Maintains stable levels of calcium and phosphorus in the bones. With a shortage of magnesium we will tend to lose flexibility, and calcium will tend to store in the blood vessel walls, making them more rigid, and consequently pushing up our blood pressure. Magnesium is a natural tranquilizer, and is the anti-stress mineral. Almost all of our magnesium is found in the vegetable kingdom, although it is fairly high in seafood, the best sources are dark green leafy produce. It is also high in soy products, such as tofu, and nuts, including almonds, Brazil, and pecans. It is also found in whole grains such as wheat, brown rice, millet, and fruits such as apricots and avocado.

Manganese - is involved in many enzyme systems to help catalyze several biochemical responses, including amino acid and energy metabolism. Manganese can take the place of magnesium in some enzyme systems. In proper amounts it can improve memory, and counteract nervousness, irritability and dizziness. In studies on rats, deficiencies of manganese led to sterility. Nuts and whole grains especially barley, whole wheat, millet and oats, although most of the manganese is found in the bran and germ of grains.

Para-amino-benzoic Acid - (PABA)is a member of the vitamin B complex, and is known for encouraging healthy hair and as a natural sun screen. It aids in the metabolization and utilization of amino acids. PABA is important to intestinal health, skin and hair pigment. It is found in wheat germ and whole grains.

Phosphorus - Forms a complex with calcium to promote proper bone and tooth mineralization. Next to calcium, phosphorus is the most abundant element in our body, is essential for energy production, protein synthesis for growth, and in the utilization of carbohydrates and fats. Seeds and nuts, whole grains,

Section Four - Food

wheat germ and bran are good vegetarian sources.

Potassium - Necessary for normal nerve transmission, blood pressure and muscle contraction. It is one of the main blood minerals known as electrolytes, the others being sodium and chloride. A diet high in potassium and lower in sodium will help prevent hypertension. The best sources are leafy green vegetables including spinach and lettuce, and vegetables such as cucumber, broccoli, lima beans, tomatoes, potatoes, and fruits including watermelon, oranges, bananas, apples, apricots, and whole grains, wheat germ, seeds, nuts.

Selenium   - Found in the anti-oxidant enzyme glutathione peroxidase, which works with Vitamin E to guard cell membranes. An important contribution to the prevention of cardiovascular disease and cancer. Barley, oats, wheat, nuts, especially Brazil, broccoli, garlic, onion, mushroom, tomato and radishes are good sources.

Sodium - is a very abundant mineral in the human body. The sodium intake for most people in our culture is way too high. About 90% of the sodium intake in the American and Canadian diets is in excess of our bodily needs. Excess can lead to high blood pressure, although the body eliminates some of the excess through sweating, urination, vomiting and diarrhea.

Excess sodium places undue stress on the kidneys. Goods natural sources are celery, seaweeds, carrots, beets and artichokes. No natural source contains an excessive amount of sodium. Most excess is consumed through processed and fast foods.

Section Four - Food

Zinc - Integral to DNA synthesis, improving acne, maintains healthy skin and cells, to support immune function increasing formation of "T" cells, assists in male sexual performance, facilitates in collagen formation, and thus it may be helpful in wound healing (150mg. Daily), and may help taste acuity. Zinc reduces oxidative damage to cell membranes.

Vegetables, Fruits, Grains and Legumes

Food should not only look, smell and taste good, it should be nutritious as well. Fresh raw fruits and vegetables are in general more nutritious than prepared or processed ones. Good food should supply our bodies with the necessary nutrients. Taste preferences, cultural mores, social customs and our own personal state of health, play a role in what we eat, how much we consume, and how often.

Proteins, Carbohydrates & Fats

Basically, proteins supply our system with the elements needed to build and repair the tissues of the body. Carbohydrates and fats supply us with the elements needed for energy. In order to reverse the aging process, the less we intake foods which have been prepared, the better.

Effects of Cooking

However, cooking certain foods can make them more palatable and in some cases even easier to digest, by inverting complex carbohydrates into simpler sugars. Unfortunately, certain elements such as vitamin C, the bioflavonoids and enzymes are destroyed by heat at relatively low temperatures and cooking times. The B vitamins which are water soluble, are not only flushed out of the body on a daily basis, and therefore need to be replaced daily, but preparing them in large amounts of water, such as is required for boiling, flushes the B vitamins out of the food, often to be flushed down the drain.

Refined Foods

Another aspect to be considered is the refining of foods. For example, grains in their whole state are composed essentially of three parts, using whole wheat as an example. These are the germ, (which is the sperm of the grain and the part where the vitamin E is located), the hull and the endosperm, which comprises the greatest part of the whole grain. The hull is indigestible, but its' presence in the system can stimulate peristaltic rhythm, which will clean out the colon. When the hull is ground up it becomes bran. Nature designed grains, which are the seeds of the earths' various grasses, to be consumed in their whole form. However, since these are foods contain life and the ability to beget life, they cannot stay on the shelf too long, otherwise the oils react with the air and become rancid. In the presence of heat, little creatures of various varieties, suddenly appear.

Effects of Refining

As a result the commercial approach is to refine whole grains by removing the germ of the grain, which is the same as castrating it, and then the hull is also removed. These elements are quite powerful from a nutritional standpoint and are fed to cattle under the name of fodda. In this refining process several important nutrients are removed including

B vitamins, vitamin E, magnesium, copper and manganese and numerous trace elements which can act as catalysts in the body, including molybdenum, selenium, silicon and zinc. Several enzymes are also lost. During the 1940s, children began developing pellagra and beri-beri which was the result of eating refined grains, and so as a result, the United States government passed laws requiring the addition of certain vitamins and minerals. This became known as *enriched flour*. Yet although there are literally dozens of elements removed, somewhere around 50+, only about eight to twelve in synthetic form are replaced.

Food Borne Illness

Another aspect to consider, especially in the new millennium is, food-borne illnesses. These are caused by the growth of the harmful bacteria. Certain guidelines should be adhered to concerning storage and preparation to help prevent food poisoning. These include cooking all meats, but in particular pork, hamburger and poultry. Always refrigerate leftovers immediately, including eggs and dairy. Avoid eating anything out of a can, but if you must on occasion, make sure the top of the can is not bulging. Botulism is deadly and cannot be killed by heating the food. Frozen foods should be cooked immediately after thawing, otherwise there is enzyme destruction. Avoid soaking fresh foods in water to prevent leeching out their water soluble elements.

Transitional Eating

As you follow the guidelines we will give you to reverse, or at least slow down your aging, you will pass through transitional eating phases. You the reader, may move through consuming a high fat standard American diet, to one that is definitely better from a nutritional and health standpoint. This should include much more fiber, and subsequently a lot more fruits and vegetables, along with a lot less fat. We the authors believe the healthiest and most youth producing nutritional regimen, is one that is vegetarian, especially a vegan vegetarian diet which contains no animal products or their derivatives, and consists of 85-90% raw foods.

We both live on such a program ourselves, using brown rice, beans, occasionally whole grain pasta, or on occasion a baked potato or baked yam. We realize that such a lifestyle will not be the goal of everyone who reads this book, but moving in such a direction will definitely improve the quality of your life and health, and life without health doesn't really have much meaning. Decide your goals!

Choose A Goal In Health

Our hope is that as our readers become healthier and more youthful. The benefits of growth in every direction will so far outweigh any downside, such as our human hedonistic tendencies might lead us to, that gradually the quality of their lifestyle choices will bring our readers to the point where they become, what they believe their ideal in life should be. Remember, what you put into your body today, won't taste as good as what it feels like to be healthy tomorrow. Supplements such as vitamins, minerals and herbals, increase your nutritional intake.

Section Four - Food

True Health

Health in the final analysis is not merely the intake of multiple nutritional elements. True health is a balance among several components, which will lead you to create a balance in your lives. The foods to be discussed in this next section are presented on an alphabetical basis, not in order of importance. *Don't be afraid to utilize color when you eat.*

Compatibility Diet

Often books on nutrition might reflect on "compatibility in diet". This is a term which refers to the eating of foods which tend to digest in a similar medium such as more alkaline or more acid. Often these treatises will say "Never mix fruits and vegetables". This is not really a hard and fast rule. There are several fruits which may be combined with vegetables, such as apples, raisins, pineapple, tomato and orange. Some people may still find such combinations incompatible. If so, avoid them.

Any reference to a physical disorder or dis-eased condition, in connection with a food or beverage, is not intended to be prescriptive. Leave that concept to those who make a living writing prescriptions. These merely represent research findings, which will be catalogued in bibliographies later on in this book.

Eggs although a good source of protein have far too much fat and cholesterol, although they do contain vitamins A, riboflavin (B_2) , D, E, niacin (B_3), copper, iron, sulphur, phosphorus and unsaturated fatty acids. Often body-builders will take raw eggs, thinking it is an improvement over the cooked. Raw eggs contain a protein called *avidin*, which can show harmful effects over an extended period of time. Avidin is de-activated by the heat of cooking. Salmonella have been known to exist in eggs, but cooking will destroy this bacterial strain.

Fiber is the only part of a natural diet that is not digested by the human body. These are the hulls of grains, as mentioned earlier and the skins of fruits. However, they do play a role in elimination. Statistically, low fiber diets have been associated with cancer of the colon and rectum, varicose veins, diverticulosis, heart disease, obesity and phlebitis.

Fish are good sources of protein, the omega 3 polyunsaturated fatty acids, iodine and potassium. Fish are of fresh water and salt water varieties. Those fish which contain the essential fatty acids are salmon and mackerel. Unfortunately, the oceans have become somewhat polluted, and even fresh water fish often contain industrial chemical elements and compounds, which are not only unhealthful but frequently carcinogenic. Shellfish are high in LDL cholesterol (the undesirable kind). Does it make any sense to subsist on food derived from a creature whose sole purpose in the scheme of Nature is to subsist on the garbage of the ocean?

The authors use organic flax seed oil for their source of the omega 3, 6, and 9, (forms of the essential fatty acids), which are an important element of a healthy regimen. Since this is a fresh, live product, it is affected by heat, light, time and air. That is why it is sold in the refrigerated section of health food stores,

Section Four - Food

in an opaque container, dated and sealed. Follow all the guidelines on the label. About two tablespoons a day is sufficient. A less expensive way is to grind the raw organic flax seeds in a coffee/nut grinder.

Vegetables

Vegetables are the mainstay of a well balanced diet. They come in an endless variety of shape, texture and flavor. Dark greens are especially high in mineral matter, in fact dark greens have twice the amount of calcium as does cows' milk, according to the U.S. governments book Composition of Foods.

Broccoli is a member of the cruciferous family, and is loaded with antioxidants. Being high in phytochemicals, it can assist in lung, breast and colon cancer. It helps to regulate blood sugar and insulin levels. It may be eaten raw or lightly steamed.

Cabbage is a hearty addition to a salad or may be used in making various slaw salads. It is antiviral, anti-ulcer and antibacterial. Because of its' high sulphur content if it is cooked by boiling, it can cause flatulence. It is loaded with phytochemicals and can speed estrogen metabolism.

Carrots are a high beta-carotene food, loaded with vitamins A and C, and high in fiber. They are believed to be effective in fighting cancer, cataracts, and macular degeneration. Carrots can also fight infection and boost immunity.

Eggplant may be used raw in salads, marinated in a good dressing or baked. Avoid eating eggplant fried. Ground up, it may also be used topically, as a skin cream. It is an antibacterial and a natural diuretic.

Section Four - Food

Kale may be used raw or in soups, is rich in antioxidants, and contains more beta-carotene and leutin, (another carotenoid), than any other vegetable. It also helps to regulate estrogen levels in the body.

Mushrooms especially shitake and tei-shi, help prevent as well as treat some cancers, lower high blood pressure, fight viral conditions such as polio and the flu, high blood cholesterol, and sticky blood platelets. Mushrooms are believed to produce an extract that is stronger than AZT in fighting AIDS. Traditionally, the kombucha mushroom is believed to strengthen the immune system, aid digestion, increase energy, and is an antitoxin.

Onions in all versions, including scallion, chive, shallot and leek, are all anti-cancer fighting agents, since they contain antioxidants. They have the ability to thin the blood, counteracting blood clots, fight atherosclerosis, lower LDL cholesterol (the bad kind), raise HDL cholesterol (the good kind), and help eliminate bronchial congestion, because of their mucus thinning properties. Onions are also antibacterial and anti-inflammatory.

Potatoes surprisingly enough are a good source of proteins, and are high in vitamins A and C, as well as thiamine (B_1), riboflavin (B_2), and niacin (B_3), and the minerals, iron, potassium, and calcium. Eaten without the additions of milk, salt and butter, potatoes can help prevent high blood pressure and stroke. They may also be eaten raw. Cooking them destroys their vitamin C content.

Section Four - Food

Pumpkin is high in vitamins A and C, loaded with beta-carotenes and other carotenoids, and contains antioxidant abilities.

Seaweeds are the vegetables of the ocean. Being such, crushed or ground, they make a great substitute for common table salt, which is a definite no-no. The authors always recommend seaweed in its' various forms for endurance athletes. There are several varieties including kelp, kombu, dulse, nori, and wakame. Each form of seaweed, all of which are loaded with a full spectrum of mineral matter, has its' own attraction. Kelp is extremely high in iodine, the vitamins E, D, K and the B complex, along with the minerals calcium and magnesium. The thinner forms such as dulse are great crumbled in salads.

Spinach is considered among the strongest of the green leafy vegetables to fight cancer, being rich in the antioxidants beta-carotene and leutin. Spinach is also high in fiber. It makes a great addition to salads, but since it is high in oxalic acid, it is best eaten raw or lightly steamed.

Yams have a much better flavor than sweet potatoes, are high in vitamins A and C and antioxidants like beta-carotene, which help prevent cataracts, heart disease, stroke and cancer.

Fruits

Fruits are great sources of vitamins and minerals, high in fiber, and the phytochemicals, and include:

Apples reduce cholesterol, stabilize blood sugar, and assist the cardiovascular, are anti-inflammatory.

Apricots are known for their tobacco/cancer fighting

ability as well as the potential to fight pancreatic cancer. *Laetrile*, a well known natural element used to combat cancer is extracted from the kernel of the apricot. Too much laetrile can be poisonous.

Bananas & Plantains are high in potassium and magnesium, and are used therapeutically in counteracting diarrhea, colitis, dyspepsia and ulcers. They are both high in natural sugars. Plantains when baked taste similar to a sweet potato.

Blueberries fight urinary tract infections, diarrhea, and they are antiviral and anti-inflammatory.

Cranberries act as a natural kidney flush, help to fight urinary tract infections, antibacterial and antiviral.

Dates are high in simple sugars, act as a natural laxative, and have been linked to lowering the chances of pancreatic cancers. Dates may be large or small, bland or super sweet, ranging from the deglet noor (sugary sweet), khawdrawi (bland-sweet), to medjool (semi-sweet).

Figs are extremely high in potassium and are great in counteracting parasites. Their high fiber/potassium content is great for intestinal elimination and alkalinizing the blood stream. Figs come in varieties including the California Black Mission, Smyrna, Calimyrna, and several middle eastern varieties.

Grapefruit as most fruit, helps unclog arteries, is anti-viral, is a natural anti-oxidant, and an anti-bacterial. It is high in vitamin C and contains the bio-flavonoids.

Grapes since the discovery of grapeseed oil, and grape skin to fight bad cholesterol and blood clotting. Grapes are also an antibiotic/antiviral.

Section Four - Food

Lemon & Lime both contain natural anti-oxidants, fight gum disease, help in sunburn and mixed with hot water and honey or maple syrup, make a good gargle for sore throats. They are natural diaphoretics (causing sweat), diuretics, and are a natural astringent.

Melons in general should be eaten alone or left alone, otherwise a major stomachache will visit. They are good blood thinners, and the orange ones contain antioxidants and beta-carotenes.

Oranges contain vitamin C and the bioflavonoids. These elements are found mainly in the white membrane under the skin. Oranges help to lower blood cholesterol, fight atherosclerosis, help in gum disease and fight arterial plaque.

Prunes which of course are dried plums, are a natural laxative due to their high oxalic acid content. They are high in fiber and may serve as a natural aspirin. In their fresh form they are antibacterial/antiviral.

Rhubarb is a natural diuretic, and can relieve constipation, since it is high in oxalic acid, so do not cook it for too long. A part of the rhubarb family is the grain known as buckwheat.

Strawberries are antiviral and antibacterial, help the cardiovascular system, are high in fiber and pectin.

Watermelon is extremely high in potassium, is antioxidant and anticoagulant, and acts as a great kidney flush. The seeds are edible.

Grains

Grains come in so many varieties including wheat, rice, barley, buckwheat, rye, corn, oats, millet, spelt, quinoa (keenwa), and triticale (trit-i-kay-lee). Each has a different flavor and texture, and although these are generally cooked before ingesting, when sprouted, they may be eaten raw in salads, mixed with greens.

They are not only among the best sources of nutrition, but also high in fiber and mineral matter, while low in fat. Whether eaten cooked or raw it is always best to sprout the grains as explained in the sprouting section of this book. Grains supply the mainstay of the worlds' food supply. When ground, grains may be used to make bread or pasta. There are different levels of flour, depending on their purpose.

Amaranth - was an ancient grain of the Central American natives, both Mayan and Aztec, and banned during the Spanish takeover of the area. There has been a resurgence of it, due to the health food movement. This high protein, high iron grain, contains calcium and B vitamins, and can be served as a grain for cereal or as a side dish to a main course. Some people like to roast it first, which inverts its' starch into a simpler sugar. As with any whole food, amaranth is high in fiber.

Barley is a hearty grain (technically a fruit) which may be used as a cereal and in soups. In some cultures barley tea is a staple, such as in Tibet, and is popular in Great Britain too. When roasted and ground it makes a beverage similar in taste to coffee, yet has no caffeine. This is extremely popular in Germany, and may be obtained at health food stores in the U.S. and Canada as a coffee substitute.

Bran is a concentrated source of B vitamins and minerals, as well as fiber. Along with its' fiber, bran

Section Four - Food

absorbs a lot of fluid which hydrates the stool that on the average diet is often too dry, due to a lack of fiber. Bran is effective in counteracting constipation, hemorrhoids, diverticulosis, speeds the metabolism of cholesterol into bile acids, and helps to counteract the ravages of heart disease, such as atherosclerosis. Sprinkle it on other cereals. Use bran in baking. Add it to cookies and loaves.

Buckwheat is not really a grain, yet is often treated as one. Originally from Russia, this is actually a member of the rhubarb family. It is pyramid shaped, dark, has a great flavor, is higher in good quality protein than any actual grain with the exceptions of oats and rice, yet unlike grains it is devoid of bran. Pilaf is made from buckwheat groats, also known as kasha. It comes in two forms; light (raw) and dark (roasted).

Bulgur is par-boiled cracked wheat, and may be used in making tabouli by marinating it in olive oil, diced onion, chopped tomato and water. Bulgur may be used in any recipe that calls for rice. It has a nutty flavor and a texture similar to cooked brown rice. It may also be used in soups, salads or as a side dish. It is also the base for couscous, a traditional middle eastern dish, made with the addition of herbs and simmered with onions.

Corn is a hearty grain, easy to prepare, is tasty, nutritious and economical. The commercial form is generally bolted or degermed, in which the sperm of the grain has been removed. Be sure to obtain only the whole grain version. Available in health food or macrobiotic stores as well as supermarket chains.

Section Four - Food

Millet may be obtained as whole kernels or in floured form. The whole grain is extremely small and can be prepared and served the same as any rice dish. It has a nutty flavor and goes well with maple syrup as a breakfast food, or can be combined with sauteed onions as a side dish, or served with a marinara.

Oat is a great grain for energy and for putting on lean weight. If you want a horse to have a beautiful coat, and lots of energy, feed it oats. Humans are no different. Oats will give a beautiful sheen to the hair when eaten. Usually we find oats in the form of rolled oats, often referred to as oatmeal. Real oatmeal is granulated or cracked. This can make a great cereal or a good addition for muffins. Refer to the section on *recipes* found later in this book. Avoid the "instant" variety of oats which are processed, have added sugar, lots of salt and preservatives.

Rice comes in several varieties.

Brown Rice is loaded with B vitamins, contains several minerals including calcium, phosphorus and iron. Brown rice also makes a good flour. **Wild Rice** contains twice the amount of protein in the form of well balanced amino acids, four times the amount of phosphorus, eight times the amount of thiamine (B_1), and twenty times as much riboflavin (B_2), as refined white rice.

White Rice also known as dehulled, refined or polished rice, is deficient in nutrients, but it may be enriched the same as white flour. **Converted Rice** is similar to white rice but a step up containing slightly more mineral matter. The authors do not recommend either of these last two for a healthy lifestyle. **Rice polish** may be bought in a health food store, and this is the part removed when making white rice. It is an easy addition to sprinkle on cereal or to add to blended drinks or when making muffins. It is high in B vitamins and mineral matter. Brown rice takes only about 30-40 minutes to prepare, and may be used as a side dish, dessert or main course.

Rye is a staple grain in Europe, where it is used in bread and rolls. It is a solid, hearty grain, with a strong flavor. It is also made into crackers called knacke, and is very popular in the Scandinavian countries. In Germany they have Hamburger Schwarzbrot or Volkornbrot, a whole grain bread. Probably the most popular form of rye bread is pumpernickel, a dark, rich flavored bread, different from anything generally found in the United States, where white flour is often used and caramel coloring is added to give a rich, dark color. Rye is an easy grain to sprout (refer to the section on sprouts earlier). Rye may be combined with peas or lentils to make a delicious pilaf. If you use rye flour it is best to grind it yourself. Make sure it is whole grain not milled or bleached.

Triticale (trit-i-kay-lee) is a grain developed by crossing wheat and rye. Many people have allergic reactions to wheat because they have been raised on cookies, bread, rolls, cereals and cake made from wheat flour, throughout their entire life. Such people often do not react to triticale in the same way. The grain is twice the size of the wheat berry. Triticale is much higher in protein than most other grains. It is rich in lysine and methionine, two amino acids which are often low in grains.

Wheat is the most common grain used in the United States and Canada. There are several forms of wheat flour. Whole grain flour retains the germ and the bran. When the germ and hull are removed before milling the flour is then called *unbleached wheat flour*.

Flour may be ground from any grain, but wheat lends itself best to the making of flour. **Bread flour** is usually made from hard winter wheat. **Pastry flour** is generally made from soft spring wheat. **Whole wheat pastry flour** is highly powdered and makes a good paste. **All purpose flour** is a blend of different refined (milled) wheat grains. **Bleached flour** is milled and then bleached white. This is what white bread is made from.

Generally in white bread, is enriched flour to which the vitamins thiamine (B_1), riboflavin (B_2), niacin (B_3) and folic acid have been added. This is what most commercial cereals are made from. The best bread of all, is that made from sprouted grains. This concept is quite old and the favorite of the ancient Essenes, writers of the Dead Sea Scrolls, two-thousand years ago. The Essenes would sprout the grains, the process of which is described earlier in this book (p.114). They would then roll the grains to crush them. This would release the gluten which is quite sticky. Buns would then be formed about the size of an open hand, and baked in the sun from sunrise until noon, and then flipped over and baked from noon until sunset. Flourless bread is the best.

Section Four - Food

The flavor & texture is unbeatable when lightly toasted. It is high in fiber, amino acids, mineral matter, and is quite filling. Unlike white fiberless bread, this Essene Bread, also known as Manna Bread will not bind the system. It comes in several varieties, and is heavy, as any good bread should be. Whole wheat berries make a good cereal but take a long time to cook. The best way to serve any grain is to sprout it.

Wheat Germ flakes may be obtained raw or lightly toasted. This is actually the sperm of the grain and contains its' vitamin E, along with calcium, potassium, magnesium and niacin.

Legumes

Legumes by definition are plants that have edible seeds within a pod. This includes peas, lentils, beans and peanuts. Legumes when sprouted are an excellent addition to salads. They contain thiamine, riboflavin, niacin, and when sprouted, the amount of vitamin C increases by 500%. The older concept that proteins to be of good quality must contain all the essential amino acids, has been debunked somewhat, but if you want to be on the more comfortable side, you can always combine legumes and grains. They complement each other perfectly, according to nutritionist, Frances Moore Lappe.

Beans are high in fiber and may be sprouted and eaten raw, or cooked and used in soups, salads, combined with brown rice, or in casseroles. They come in numerous varieties including kidney, black eye, aduki (adzucki), soy, black, lima, pinto, white, garbanzo and navy. They are inexpensive, and in their dry form can be stored for years in a cool, dry atmosphere, which far outweighs the standard five varieties of meat plus poultry commonly available in the Western hemisphere. They are good sources of protein, devoid of cholesterol, and are low in fat.

Peas may be used as a side dish, sprouted and added to salads, or made into soup. They are said to be a natural contraceptive. Dried peas may keep for a long time, especially if kept in a cool, dry, place. Some people like to add baking soda, but this will destroy thiamine (B_1).

Soybeans are also high in fiber and extremely versatile in making other foods such as tofu and so-called meat substitutes. They are high in the phyto-estrogens, and may be used in place of estrogen in some menopausal women.

Soybeans help regulate blood sugar, the bowels, and lower cholesterol. They are also high in vitamins and minerals, especially in the B vitamins, calcium, phosphorus, magnesium, potassium, iron and zinc.

Ground into flour and adding water and oil, soybeans may be made into soy milk and soy cream. Soy flour can even be prepared to look and taste like scrambled eggs. Soy is also high in isoflavones, which convert to phyto-estrogens and fight hormonal cancers such as prostate and breast cancer. Soy oil is high in linoleic acid, an essential fatty acid, necessary for humans. Soy milk is often used for children who cannot handle cows' milk. Japanese and macrobiotic recipes use items such as tempeh, which is a fermented nutty flavored patty. Miso is a paste made from fermented soybeans and some grain such as barley or rice. After the soybeans and grain have been fermented together, the resultant paste is squeezed through a cheesecloth, and the solid matter is miso, which is used as a base for soup. The remaining fluid is called tamari or soy sauce. Commercial soy sauce is made with water, caramel coloring, sugar, salt and monosodium glutamate (q.v. in the **Additives** section). The flavor and quality of the natural is far superior. Soy is the base for textured vegetable protein.

Herbals/Spices/Condiments

At the beginning of each recipe section there will be a list of herbals, spices and condiments which may be added to any of the recipes within that section.

Following is an outline of most of the herbs that might be used, since we realize that many of our readers may not be familiar with them. First, explanations and definitions, then, an herbal glossary.

Spices and Condiments were originally used to cover the taste of foods as they began to ferment or go bad, developing an off taste. This was helpful in hot climates with no other means of preserving. In areas of the planet where there was a lot of moisture, usually fermentation was the developed form of preserving. In desert atmospheres things were preserved through dehydration or drying, hot tropical or semi-tropical atmospheres used hot spices.

As travel became more in vogue, other qualities of spice became commonplace such as hot, sweet, salty, bitter and sour. A basic rule in using spices and condiments is "less is better". It is easy to overdo when adding condiments. More can always be added by individuals according to their own taste. When using fresh instead of dried condiments, use three to four (3-4) times the amount specified, since in the dry form, herbs are much more concentrated.

Herbal Teas contain elements that can heal and even prevent several common conditions. Many prescription drugs are resourced from the elements in herbs. Always check with a professional knowledgeable in herbal compounds. Be aware that *chamomile, goldenrod, yarrow* and *marigold* will on occasion cause allergic reactions. Be especially careful of chrysanthemum, ragweed and asters. Nutmeg, juniper, the leaves of senna and aloe, dock root and buckthorn bark can cause diarrhea in some people.

Unusual Foods

allspice - although its' name appears to be a combination of several spices, allspice is a simple berry, usually dried and ground. It has a sharp flavor with a hint of cinnamon and clove. It is generally used in baked dessert dishes.

anise - its' flavor is sweet and spicy, and it has a licorice like flavor. This makes it a welcome addition in baked goods and some drinks. It has been used in Asian food dishes for centuries. For a change, add a teaspoon of anise seed to salad dressing.

basil - basil gives a slight clove like flavor, and may be added to soups, salad dressings, stews and vegetables. Its' flavor doubles when it is cooked.

bay leaf - is an important ingredient in *bouquet garni* used in stuffing, which traditionally contains two parts parsley, two parts chervil, one part thyme, one part marjoram and one-half part bay leaf. This is because the flavor of bay leaf multiplies as it cooks. It is best to place the bay leaf in an herb bag while cooking so that it may be removed after the flavor is imparted, since bay does not soften while cooking.

caraway - is used all over the world, forms the basis for a good herbal salad, and makes a good addition to rye bread. It makes a great addition to apple dishes.

chili peppers - not all chilis are super hot, some are relatively mild, while others are sweet. They are used for stews and pickling, but recent studies have revealed that the super hot chilis actually burn the mucosa in the throat, which is later replaced by scar tissue, which is why gradually the strength of the chilis must be increased in order to get that bite again.

chives - are often indispensable for many cooks. They may be used in salads and on raw vegetable platters. They are sometimes used in soups, sandwiches and sauces, but are best consumed raw.

cinnamon - may be used in a number of unexpected ways, for instance in Greece and Armenia, cinnamon is a standard ingredient in tomato sauce. This particular spice is strong, so go lightly. It may be used in vegetable or fruit dishes, in sweet potato, winter squash, fresh pineapple, muffins or pudding. It can be obtained in stick form or as a powder.

clove - The most easily identified spice can be used in holiday dishes whether vegetable, fruit or grain. It is derived from a dried bud and is available in whole or ground form. It makes a nice addition to apple juice, fruit punch, herbal teas, apples, peaches or beets.

dill - makes a great addition to salads, although it is just as popular in fermented items such as is found in pickling cucumbers. Both the herb and the seed are used, and in its' ground state, dill may be added to tofu spreads, to add a delicate flavor. A lot may be used without fear of overpowering the general flavor of the main items. Allow some dill to marinate in an olive oil, apple cider vinegar combo, for a unique salad dressing. This can help make simple fare more palatable.

fennel - or finocchio as the Italians call it, may be used in almost any kind of prepared dish. The stalks can be served raw in a snack, or as an augmentation to appetizers or salads. The seeds flavor is similar to anise. Add to herbal teas, muffins or crackers.

garlic - has been used for so long that it is mentioned in the ancient Hebrew Talmudic Law, employed by the Babylonians as far back as 3,000 B.C.E. (Before Current Era the new designation for B.C.), and was used by the Chinese at least 1,000 B.C.E.

The ancient Hebrews were required to use garlic in certain dishes and on specific occasions. It makes a great base when a cut petal is rubbed on the inside of a salad bowl. Diced and sauteed with olive oil and onion, it makes a great base for sauce.

Four crushed petals may be combined with soy "butter" (found in the **Recipes** section of this book), to make an unusual spread. Raw it can be used in a number of dishes especially salads. Chewing on

Section Four - Food

a sprig of parsley will cancel out garlic breath. This overcomes the stigma some have to avoid it.

ginger - root may be used in a variety of dishes that range from appetizers to main dishes. It makes a nice ingredient to add to sauces and desserts, especially in Asian style foods. It may be added to apple, peach, carrot, onion and legume dishes. It can be used as a fresh root or in shredded, dried or powdered forms. In its' dry form it should be kept in a tightly covered jar to prevent it from losing its' flavor. It is quite strong, so at first go lightly with it.

marjoram - has a sweet, strong, yet slight spicy flavor. It makes a good addition to grain loaves, and is good when one is weaning themselves off of meat dishes. Marjoram can easily overpower other flavors, so it should be used sparingly. Chopped and mixed with soy "butter", it makes a nice spread on whole grain toast or toasted Essene or Manna bread.

mint - comes in several versions. Among the most popular are spearmint and peppermint. During the heat of summer hanging a fresh bunch of mint to impart aroma to a room also gives a hint of coolness to an otherwise hot atmosphere. Mint in its' various forms may be used as a tea, natural jams, in sauces, mixed in a salad, or combined with olive oil and apple cider vinegar. Mint can also combine well with beets, spinach, potatoes and with several legumes.

mustard - adds a slightly spicy flavor to cooked dishes, sauces, dressings and salads. Mustard works with potato, pickled cucumbers, celery preparations.

nutmeg - is indispensable in traditional holiday

Section Four - Food

desserts. Nutmeg can be added to squash, pumpkin, carrot, beet or apple dishes, including apple sauce or other fruit sauces. It can be used whole or ground.

oregano - is a welcome addition to tomato based sauces, and whole grain pasta dishes. Oregano imparts a zesty aroma and a slightly sharp flavor to both salads and sauces, whether used fresh or dry.

rosemary - is fragrant, sweet and savory. It makes a nice addition to natural jams, and adds a uniqueness to tofu, sauteed in a little olive oil. Be careful to not overdo. Rosemary has an ability to overpower.

sage - sometimes comes across as overpowering but can be toned down with parsley. As with rosemary, this condiment should be used with caution. Sage can add a special stroke to fruit drinks/dishes and salads.

tarragon - is identified with more sophisticated dishes. Chopped it can be used in dressing, however if too much is used, it gives a little bite to the flavor. Fill a wide-mouthed jar with apple cider vinegar, and drop in twigs of fresh tarragon. It goes especially well with cauliflower, and a home made tartar sauce.

thyme - can easily overpower more delicate herbs, and can serve as a digestive aid. It gives a nice touch to thick soups (split pea, minestrone, lentil or bean).

Herbal Glossary

The following terms refer to the action of many herbals. As you explore the world of herbs, the following terms should serve as an herbal guide.

Alterative - The ability to alter or in some way change a condition. Alteratives also purify the blood.

Analgesic - Relieves pain by acting as a nervine,

Section Four - Food

counter irritant that causes a reddening of the skin, antibiotic, antiseptic, antispasmodic.

Anodyne - Pain reliever.

Antibiotic - The ability to kill or inhibit bacterial growth of organisms.

Antidote - A substance which counteracts another, especially a poisonous substance.

Antiperiodic - Preventing the periodic return of diseased states.

Antiseptic - The ability to destroy infection causing microorganisms.

Antispasmodic - Relieving or preventing involuntary muscle spasms or cramps.

Aperient - A mild gently acting laxative.

Aromatic - Substance with a spicy scent and pungent yet pleasant taste, used as a fragrance.

Astringent - Tightens & contracts the skin or tissues. Inhibits the discharge of blood and mucous.

Calmative - A substance that lessens excitement. This is generally lower in strength than a sedative.

Carminative - Checking the formation of gas, while helping to dispel what gas has already formed.

Cholagogue - Promoting the discharge of bile.

Demulcent - Mucilaginous, soothes the intestines.

Deobstruent - clears obstructions from body ducts.

Depurative - removes waste, purifies the blood.

Detergent - Has a cleansing action.

Diaphoretic - Can promote sweating.

Diuretic - Promotes the flow of urine.

Emetic - A substance that induces vomiting.

Emmenagogue - Promoting menstruation.

Section Four - Food

Emollient - A substance that softens the skin.

Expectorant - Anything that helps the body expel phlegm through spitting, sneezing or coughing.

Flatulence - Gas in the stomach or bowels.

Hemostatic - Checks internal bleeding.

Hepatic - Anything that affects the liver.

Laxative - To promote bowel movement.

Mucilaginous - Soothing for inflamed parts.

Nervine - Calming irritation from strain or fatigue.

Pectoral - Relieving ailments of the lung or chest

Purgative - Has the power to evacuate the intestines.

Refrigerant - Reduces fevers, has a cooling effect.

Scrofula - Infection & inflammation of lymph.

Sedative - The ability to calm the nerves.

Stimulant - Increasing or quickening various functions of the body, such as digestion or appetite. The difference between a stimulant and a tonic is, a tonic takes time.

Stomachic - Toning & strengthening the stomach.

Tonic - Invigorating or strengthening the system.

Vasodilator - Ability to expand the blood vessels.

Vermifuge - Destroys and helps expel worms.

Vesicant - Causes blisters or sores, (poison ivy).

Vulnerary - An application for external wounds.

Irradiation of Food

Irradiation is a method of food preservation in which foods are treated with low doses of gamma radiation from Cobalt 60 or the radio-active isotope Cesium 137, a by-product of nuclear weapon production and nuclear power generation. It may also be done by X-ray or high voltage electron to kill bacteria and parasites, to delay sprouting or to increase shelf life.

When food is irradiated, nutrients are destroyed and compounds called URPs (unique radiolytic products) are created. These are feared to be powerful carcinogens. The long term effects of these residual elements is unknown at this time.

Irradiation is also known as "*ionizing radiation*", because it produces energy waves strong enough to alter atoms and molecules, converting them into electrically charged particles called ions. Ionizing radiation reduces the number of disease causing organisms in foods by killing them. This is also known as "cold pasteurization" and "irradiation pasteurization".

The United States Food and Drug Administration (FDA) and the United States Department of Agriculture have allowed the use of irradiation since the early 1960s. In 1963 the FDA approved the use of radiation to kill pests in wheat and flour. In 1985 they approved the irradiation of pork to control the parasites that cause trichinosis. The following year they approved this same process to delay the maturation, and to disinfect and inhibit the growth in vegetables and spices. In 1992 the USDA approved the use of irradiation of raw poultry to kill salmonella and similar bacterial strains. Finally, in 1997, the FDA approved the irradiation of red meats.

There is actually a rising need for control over this ever growing list of pathogens such as E. coli and salmonella. This is due in part to the intake of

Section Four - Food

more raw foods as well as in importing of foods from other countries, which do not always have higher standards in their growing methods. Another aspect to be considered is the lack of awareness or caring when it comes to safe handling practices.

The Executive Director of the Center for Science In the Public Interest, Michael Jacobson, criticized irradiation as recent as December 1997, describing it as a high-tech "end of the line" solution to contamination problems that should have been addressed earlier.

Irradiation can only help control the contamination once it occurs; it cannot prevent it. Even those who are willing to try it, say it is "...no match for bad sanitation and substandard practices", as quoted by Osterholm and Potter, in the periodical Emerging Infectious Disease 1997.

One argument in favor of irradiation of foods is that it can kill or at least substantially reduce the number of harmful organisms found in food, and it can kill insects infesting food stuffs such as grains and their by products without leaving chemical residues. In fact the estimates of those creatures killed runs in the 90% range. Another claim is that it can sterilize foods for immune compromised people such as those with HIV or AIDS.

On the flip side of the coin irradiation as now recommended will not eradicate all pathogens. Those which survive are termed "radiation resistant". Another aspect of the down side is that we may create super strains of pathogens, which will create new problems. The present allowable level of radiation is ineffective against the Norwalk virus which is found in seafood. Certain foods such as tomato, grape, lettuce and cucumbers become mushy and/or not palatable after being irradiated.

Irradiation delays sprouting and ripening, which allows food to be stored longer, but that is probably because it is damaging or destroying the life of the plant. Of course a longer shelf life provides a major benefit to the food processors.

There are certain nutrient losses that should also be taken into consideration including a 25% reduction in vitamin E, decreases in thiamin (vitamin B1), and a 5-10% reduction in vitamin C. The FDA originally required labels if the ingredients represented more than 90% of the total product. By law these labels were to prominently display the radiation logo, known as the "radura", and accompanied by the words "treated with irradiation". The Food and Drug Administration Modernization Act of 1997 (FDAMA), section 306 allowed that the "required irradiation disclosure statement...no longer need be any more prominent than the declaration of the ingredients".

There are too many unanswered questions the long term safety of irradiation. Since irradiation can only be used on a very limited number of foods, it is not really practical to expect to eliminate the challenge of preventing contamination completely.

There are practical alternatives to irradiating our food. One approach is Hazard Analysis Critical Control Point (HACCP). Then there is also pulsed

Section Four - Food

light, ozone treatment and high pressure. None of these are fully developed at this time, they could provide viable alternatives. Such programs can provide long term control of food borne bacteria and viruses without the possible dangers or undesirable aspects of irradiation.

As consumers we can voice our concerns to federal legislators. We have the right to know whether or not the foods we are buying are safe or exposed to radiation. As a concerned person you can also contact the USDA Food Safety and Inspection Service at 1-800-535-4555 or the FDA at 1-800-FDA-4010, and let these agencies know how you feel.

The New Food Pyramid

According to a coalition of consumer and health groups, Americans are not eating enough fruits and vegetables. As reported in several Newspapers across the nation in February 1999, representatives of more than twenty major organizations including the *American Heart Association*, the *American Association of Retired Persons* (AARP), and the *American Cancer Society* urged the federal government to revamp the present food pyramid and make fruits and vegetables the center of the ideal American diet in the forthcoming revised nutritional guidelines.

According to Elizabeth Pivonka, President of the *Produce for Better Health Foundation,* "We are suffering and sometimes dying from a fruit and vegetable deficit that is growing larger everyday. Taking a pill will not make up for this deficit".

The Dietary Guidelines Committee

The *Dietary Guidelines Committee* which includes top nutritionists from several universities, as well as top officials from the Department of Agriculture and from the Department of Health and Human Services, was scheduled to release new guidelines in the year 2000.

The foundation and the other groups want the pyramid revised so that they show fruits and vegetables at the base of the recommended diet.

Pivonka, a nutritionist, further said "As the guidelines stand now, they do include fruits and vegetables, but simply including them is not enough. We are petitioning the federal government to emphasize fruits and vegetables, not just as part of a balanced diet, but as the core of it."

The structure of the pyramid at present, which is a vast improvement over the previous version where animal derived foods were the most important aspect of a nutritionally sound program, has grains as the basis of the structure, with fruits and vegetables at the second level, superceded by dairy, meat, nuts, beans and legumes.

The current guidelines advise five daily servings of fruit and vegetables, yet according to Pivonka, Americans still do not eat enough of these items. Pivonka said that studies show "We are more likely to start the day with coffee as with fruit juice. We found that only 17% of the food we eat at lunch are fruits, vegetables or 100% juice." Pivonka further states, "Four of the top six causes of death in the United

States are diet related. These include heart disease, stroke, cancer and diabetes."

Cornell University Research

Colin Campbell of New York's Cornell University, who for the past thirty plus years has conducted an extensive study of countries which have low levels of the debilitating diseases such as heart attack, stroke, hypertension and cancer, has found that in places like China and southern Italy where much of the caloric content is derived from vegetables, whole grains and fish, that the incidence of these killer diseases is extremely low. Campbell has stated that people can derive all the nutrients they need from a plant based dietary regimen. In actuality he said, "There are no essential nutrients in animal based foods that are not also available to better advantage, in properly grown plant based foods." His research is explored earlier.

Cost Saving

From a purely health oriented standpoint, not only is a good vegetarian regimen better for people, but the cost saved in insurance and hospitalization alone will bring about a quantum shift from the present concept of what health is.

American Cancer Society

According to Dr. David Rosenthal, immediate past president of the American Cancer Society, "The evidence is very strong that those who eat five or more servings of fruit and vegetables daily, are at a lower risk of cancer." He further said, "While one third of all cancers are related to tobacco use, another third are related to diet. We showed that we could do it with tobacco, the same cultural change has to take place with eating."

A behavioral scientist at the University of Texas Anderson Cancer Center, Karen Webber-Cullen said, "That the right food is often available, but not in the form most people want to eat it. I doubt that most kids go into a fast food restaurant and order a salad. Why do we need a double cheeseburger? I'd like to see a double tomato burger!"

Herbs for Anti-Aging

During the 1990's a whole spectrum of anti-aging substances suddenly came to light. Many have exotic names such as kava-kava or ginkgo biloba, and many are also tried and true when it comes to their efficacy. We are going to explore several, some of which are minerals or combinations of amino acids and minerals, others are simple herbal supplements.

Herbs and Other Natural Supplements

Please Note: *The information in this section of the book is not intended to replace the services of a trained and qualified professional in the healing arts. Self medication of ill health without competent assistance could be harmful or dangerous.*

Herbs have been used for thousands of years to address the physical complaints or increase the well being of people all over the world, throughout every developed culture. Interest in herbs and other supplements has grown in recent years. As with vitamin supplements, there is an ongoing debate in the scientific community about the value of taking herbs and non-vitamin supplements.

Section Four - Food

Many scientific studies touting benefits have been conducted in other countries with a longer history of herb use than the United States has had. The results of scientific studies are extremely promising. Many of these herbs and supplements are widely recommended by doctors throughout Europe.

Please remember that intelligent, informed self care includes consulting the health professionals that you trust the most as part of educating yourself and taking responsibility for your own health and that of your family. Because people have individual responses to herbs and supplements, or because you may be taking medication that might be affected by the simultaneous consumption of herbs and supplements, consult your health care provider before you begin taking any new or untried herbs and supplements. *If you are pregnant or nursing, or if you wish to give supplements to your children, please check with a primary care healer who has experience in this field first. Not all primary care healers have either the necessary training or experience.*

General Guidelines

The directions listed on each bottle of most herbs and supplements in general, represent the supplier's best recommendation for the average person. If you have never taken the supplement before, you may want to begin with smaller amounts than those listed, to gauge your personal reaction to it. Do not exceed the recommended directions unless you are working closely with a knowledgeable health care provider who can monitor your response.

Section Four - Food

As with any crop, herbs grown in different regions or different years may have differences in content, that's why, whenever possible, it is important to check on the characterizing ingredient that must appear in the supplement. A *characterizing ingredient* is the component believed to confer its benefits.

Standardizing these ingredients makes sure that each batch of product contains the same level of the characterizing ingredient. It is the only way of ensuring that each tablet or capsule has a known and consistent level of potency. Herbs and supplements are usually assayed to ensure that they contain the stated potency. Following is a list of common supplements including their Latin designation, their action in the body, and their reported uses.

Acidophilus

Characterizing Ingredient: Lactobacillus acidophilus: several millions per capsule.

Actions: Your colon is populated with many types of bacteria. Some are beneficial, others are not; the friendly bacteria help keep the unfriendly ones in check. Lactobacillus acidophilus is a friendly bacteria. It converts some lactose (milk sugar) into lactic acid. It is one of the active cultures in yogurt.

Reported Uses: May help maintain the health of the digestive tract. May be helpful for people with lactose intolerance; may be useful in reintroducing friendly bacteria into the intestine after antibiotic use.

Aloe (Aloe Vera, Liliaceae)

Aloe is best known for its' healing ability for burns,

Section Four - Food

scalds, radiation, excessive sun exposure, abrasions, infections, lacerations and poison ivy. It has anti-bacterial, anesthetic, as well as tissue restorative properties. It may also be used on blistered skin and to relieve cold sores. Aloe tends to deteriorate after exposure to the atmosphere. In work one of your authors' researched in Mexico, with many indigenous peoples, a leaf of Aloe combined with a crushed or blended apple or unfiltered apple juice, using enough apple to make the combination palatable, would stop dysentery within twenty to thirty minutes.

Chamomile (Anthemis nobilis Matricaria camomilla) *Actions:* stomachic, tonic, anti-inflammatory, vermifuge and anti-bacterial.

Chamomile, known for it's apple-like fragrance, is an immune stimulator. It is helpful in healing ulcers, upset stomach, headache and hysteria. Chamomile tea has been known to relieve the inflammation of arthritic and rheumatic discomfort. It is also recognized for relieving menstrual cramps and in killing vaginal yeast. The tea is widely known as a relaxant and to induce sleep. When sponged on the body and left to dry it may also be used as an insect repellent. Large amounts (over 3 cups daily), have been known to cause nausea and at times vomiting.

Chromium Picolinate

When deciding whether or not to take any supplement, there are three questions you should ask: Is it safe? Is it effective? Do I need it?

An essential trace mineral, chromium is required by our body in very small amounts - estimated to be about 50 to 200 mcg (micrograms) per day. Chromium is best known for its role in the metabolism of glucose. Research shows that it may improve the ability of glucose intolerant people to remove excess sugar from their blood after eating.

The typical American diet which is dominated by processed foods is low in chromium containing foods, such as brewer's yeast and whole grains. In the book, The Chromium Program, Jeffrey a. Fisher M.D., says that the average diet is not only low in chromium, but is chromium robbing, since consuming processed foods depletes the body's chromium supply, and the chromium containing foods we do eat may be grown in "low chromium soil."

In recent years, some people have chosen to supplement their diets with chromium, often in the form of either chromium picolinate (chromium bonded to picolinate) or chromium polynicotinate (chromium bonded to niacin). Both are designed to make the chromium more absorbable in the body.

Gary Evans, Ph.D. in an interview with Better Nutrition, said that chromium picolinate has been tested for mutagenesis by using a well acknowledged method, known as the Ames Test; a test for screening chemicals to determine whether or not they are mutagenic. Evans also believes that other research, in particular, that conducted by well-known chromium researcher, Richard A. Anderson, Ph.D. has shown chromium picolinate to be both safe and effective.

The Washington, D.C. based *Council for Responsible Nutrition* also gave chromium picolinate

Section Four - Food

the OK in a recent issue of its CRN News Supplement, saying, "Numerous studies in animals and humans support the safety of chromium picolinate. DNA experiments performed with bacteria and rats concluded that this compound does not cause chromosome damage."

Coenzyme Q10 (Ubiquinone)

Characterizing Ingredient: Coenzyme Q10

Reported uses: Besides being part of the energy chain in your cells, Co-enzyme Q10 is believed to function as an antioxidant in lipoprotein tissue (Lipoprotein is the last "L" in LDL and HDL cholesterol) and to help stabilize cell membranes. It may work alone or as a back up for vitamin E.

Reported Uses: low circulating levels of Co-enzyme Q10 have been found in persons with heart disease. Studies show supplementation with Co-enzyme Q10 has improved heart function in patients.

Coenzyme Q10 is an essential element of the mitochondria. These are the energy producing section of the cells of the body. It is involved in the manufacture of ATP (adrenotriphosphate), the energy component of all body processes. The human body cannot function very well without a good supply of Coenzyme Q10. Deficiencies may lead to heart conditions and in severe cases even heart failure. Coenzyme Q10 levels generally are reduced as we go through the aging process.

This element is used mainly in the treatment of cardiovascular diseases, such as high blood pressure, cardio-myopathy, angina, congestive heart

Section Four - Food

failure and mitral valve prolapse. Along with heart conditions, Coenzyme Q10 is also used to treat immune deficiency disorders, enhancing athletic performance, periodontal conditions, weight and diabetes.

According to Folkers, Vadhanavikit and Mortensen in a paper for the *National Academy of Sciences* state that biopsy results from heart tissue in patients with various cardiovascular diseases showed a Coenzyme Q10 deficiency in 50-75% of the cases. Diglesi, Langsjoen and others in papers done as recently as 1994 state that Coenzyme Q10 has been shown to lower blood pressure in patients with high blood pressure, within two to three months after inception. A deficiency of this nutrient was found in four out of ten patients with high blood pressure.

Bliznakov, Mayer and others back in the seventies refer to Coenzyme Q10 as an enhancer of the immune system. It has also been shown that people who are obese are deficient in Coenzyme Q10. The general dosage is between 50 to 150 mg. daily, although for more severe cases 150-300 mg. per day. It has been found to be synergistic with more elements than any other substance intake, although the usual cautions should apply with pregnant and lactating women, unless suggested by their primary care healer.

Echinacea
Characterizing Ingredients: (Echinacea purpurea and Echinacea angustifolia, Compositae)

Section Four - Food

Reported uses: Studies have shown echinacea stimulates phagocytosis (in which cells destroy invading bacteria and viruses) and increases mobility of leukocytes and other white blood cells important in maintaining our bodies' defense mechanisms.

Reported Uses: Studies have backed its usage in maintaining the health of the immune system.

Echinacea is best known for its immune stimulant properties and for infectious conditions, colds, flu, and boils. The roots are used for a tonic and as a blood purifier, bee stings, eczema, snakebite, tumors, hemorrhoids and streptococcal infections. It tends to knit the skin and prevent bacteria from penetrating the tissue.

It is an antibiotic and anti-inflammatory for arthritic conditions. It also helps to preserve the white blood cells during radiation therapy.

Enzymes

What are you dealing with health wise? Premature wrinkles, digestive troubles, high cholesterol levels, atherosclerosis? If so, chances are you have enzyme deficiencies! Enzymes are the catalysts of the human body, and they make metabolism possible. Best known for their roles in digestion, enzymes are responsible for every function that takes place in your body. During every moment of our lives, over 3,000 different enzymes are constantly renewing and changing, often at unbelievable speed.

Each enzyme promotes specific reactions. Protease breaks proteins into smaller molecules, amylase splits carbohydrates (starches and sugars),

Section Four - Food

and lipase breaks down fats, while antioxidant enzymes, such as catalase, superoxide dismutase, and glutathione peroxidase, all fight free radicals. Other enzymes are responsible for storage and release of energy, aid respiration, help in reproduction, and improve vision.

An enzyme shortage may lead to imbalances, which could eventually lead to disease. For example, people with lactose intolerance lack the enzyme lactase needed to break down lactose, the di-saccharide sugar in milk, so they must avoid all dairy products; or they may be helped by taking lactase enzymes. But lactase only works on lactose, not on other substances, such as the milk protein, casein, an equal cause of concern. This is due to the fact that enzymes are so specific.

Poor digestion is one of the first signs of an enzyme deficiency. Another indicator of an enzyme shortage that is not as easy to see, since its effects are at the cellular level, is free radical formation. Wrinkling is the most obvious sign of this process occurring. The antioxidant enzymes fight the free radicals that destroy our bodies from the outside and the inside.

Enzymes and Heat

Traditionally, foods have been the primary source for enzymes; however, the heat of cooking foods above 180 degrees, can kill enzymes. Uncooked foods (such as fruits and vegetables) are usually high in enzyme activity, unless they have been treated with preservatives or food additives, held in storage for long periods, or irradiated, dried, or frozen.

Section Four - Food

Even if you're eating an optimal diet, you might need enzyme supplements if you have a problem digesting or absorbing the nutrients in your foods.

Available in tablets, capsules, or powder, most enzymes are taken orally, and can be found in your local health food store. However, some enzyme products can be taken sublingually (under the tongue) which allows the substance to be more easily absorbed, topically (in ointment form), or by other means, in more serious cases. Enzymes are necessary for everything that happens in your body. Enzymes are the catalysts of life.

Evening Primrose Oil

Characterizing Ingredient: Gamma-Linolenic Acid (GLA): *Reported uses:* Prostaglandin E1, a metabolite involved in the inflammatory response, is made from GLA. May aid in reducing atopic (skin) and other types of inflammation; studies have shown both positive and negative results. Some women find it useful when taken in the days prior to menstruation.

Garlic (Odorless)

Characterizing Ingredient: Equivalent to 1,200 milligrams of garlic per tablet (400-mg concentrate); four milligrams allicin potential.

Reported uses: Allicin has antibacterial properties and also forms a compound called ajoene, which is believed to prevent platelet aggregation, thereby reducing blood clotting.

Reported Uses: Studies have shown that garlic has antibacterial effects, can reduce blood cholesterol, and may support cardiovascular health. Garlic a member of the onion family, and has been used to combat bacteria and parasites. It is a good decongestant and expectorant. It contains several antioxidants, is an antispasmodic, lowers cholesterol, blood pressure & is anti-inflammatory.

Ginkgo Biloba
Characterizing Ingredient: derived from leaves.
Reported uses: Those with blood clotting disorders should avoid using ginkgo. A vasodilator and free radical scavenger, the characterizing ingredients in ginkgo are associated with improved blood flow and increased oxygen metabolism, especially in the arteries and capillaries in the brain. This is not recommended for those on blood thinning meds.

Widely recommended for poor circulation, short term memory loss, headache, tinnitis (ringing in the ears) and several other related disorders. It is used to treat deafness, impotence, stroke, heart disease and aging, as well as for asthma, and prevent inebriation from alcohol. It is also used for vertigo, high blood pressure, allergies and impotence.

Among the side effects are nausea, irritability, diarrhea, vomiting and restlessness.

Ginseng (Korean)
Characterizing Ingredient: Ginsenosides (triterpenoid saponins):
Actions: It is thought to have stimulative properties.
Reported Uses: stimulant, sedative, mild laxative, diaphoretic, tonic, stomachic and alterative. Ginseng is used for many reasons, but the most commonly agreed upon use is as a general tonic. Ginseng is

Section Four - Food

called an adaptogen (qv.). In the Western world, ginseng strengthens the immune system and bodily functions; helps sufferers adapt to mental, emotional and physical stress and for stamina and energy.

In traditional Chinese medicine (TCM), ginseng is used for many purposes, including regulating blood pressure and blood sugar, as a sexual tonic for both men and women, and to strengthen overall health when the body is run down.

In laboratory studies, ginseng has shown potential in protecting liver and heart health, regulating the function of reproductive hormones, normalizing cholesterol and blood sugar levels, and improving memory and learning. Taking large doses of ginseng in combination with stimulants, including caffeine, is not recommended. Ginseng is best avoided by those with high blood pressure and during pregnancy.

Goldenseal

Reported uses: laxative, tonic, alterative, antiseptic, periodic and diuretic.

Goldenseal has a positive effect on the mucus membranes, and is helpful in catarrhal conditions, whether oral, nasal or intestinal. It is a tonic for spinal nerves, helps in digestive biliousness and leucorrhea. It also helps with ulcerations of the mouth, stomach and bowels, and may be used in dysentery and diarrhea. It may also relieve nausea during pregnancy. A douche of goldenseal can help sooth vaginal and uterine inflammations. It may also be used on open sores and skin conditions. Those with hypoglycemia and hypertension should avoid using it internally.

Section Four - Food

Goldenseal tea may help relieve pyorrhea and sore gums when brushed on these areas. Those suffering from high blood pressure, heart disease, stroke, diabetes or glaucoma, should not use this.

Grape Seed Extract

Characterizing Ingredient: Proanthocyanidin:

Actions: Proanthocyanidins have antioxidant effects.

Reported Uses: May reduce oxidation of lipoproteins. Oxidation of lipoproteins is believed to be one of the first steps in the formatting of cholesterol plaque (hardening of the arteries).

According to a recent Japanese study reported in <u>Atherosclerosis</u> magazine, a small amount of grapeseed extract added to the diets of animals prevented a certain form of heart disease known as aortic atherosclerosis. This research may well apply to humans as well.

Grapeseed extract is rich in a class of polyphenols, known as proanthocyanidins. These were added to the food of the rabbits in the study. Researchers found that although the grapeseed did not affect the rabbits serum cholesterol levels, it did lower considerably the cholesterol in the wall of the aorta, the major artery carrying oxygenized blood away from the heart.

Typically in the case of atherosclerosis, the smooth muscle cells show oxidation. The aortic walls of the rabbits fed grapeseed oil did not. Researchers suggest taking grapeseed oil extract in doses of about 1.25 grams per day for a person at 110 pounds.

Section Four - Food

Hawthorn (Crataegus oxyacantha)
Reported uses: sedative, anti-spasmodic, vasodilator

Cardiac disease kills people. In fact, despite untold advances in surgical techniques, and pharmaceutical medications, cardiovascular disease remains the number one cause of death in America. Heart disease is, in large part, controllable.

A healthy diet, low in animal and saturated fats, lots of water, and regular exercise can keep your vessels well.

One of the things that many herbs do quite well is improve circulation. Among the best, is hawthorn. Hawthorn is rich in flavonoids, anthocyanidins and proanthocyanidins. Flavonoids are what give red wine its benefit for heart disease.

European studies have confirmed hawthorn to be most effective for the following cardiac conditions: angina, myocardial weakness, arrhythmia, and congestive heart failure. Patients with congestive heart failure note improvement in five areas: endurance, shortness of breath, ankle edema, nighttime urination, and mental and emotional well being.

Herbal Teas

Herbal teas contain elements that can heal and even prevent several common conditions. Many prescription drugs are resourced from the elements in herbs. Always check with a professional knowledgeable in herbal compounds. Be aware that chamomile, goldenrod, yarrow and marigold will on occasion cause allergic reactions. Be especially careful of chrysanthemum, ragweed and asters. Nutmeg, juniper, the leaves of senna and aloe, dock root and buckthorn bark can cause diarrhea.

Lecithin

Characterizing Ingredient: Phosphatidylcholine

Actions: Lecithin, or phosphatidylcholine, are an important part of cell membranes, lipoproteins (part of LDL and HDL cholesterol), and the lining of the lung. It is also involved in nerve transmission.

Lecithin helps to metabolize fat in the body and aids in the digestion and absorption of fats. It is found in soy beans, nuts, unrefined vegetable oils, whole wheat and corn. Lecithin also helps to break up cholesterol deposits and pass it through the arterial walls, thus helping to prevent atherosclerosis. It also helps to prevent the formation of gallstones, purify the kidneys and cleanse the liver. Suggested two tablespoons daily.

Omega 3 Fatty Acids

Characterizing Ingredient: EPA (Eicosapentaenoic Acid); DHA (Docasahexaenoic Acid)

Actions: Omega 3 fatty acids, the unique type of fat found in fish, and the oils of certain seeds, have been shown to reduce platelet aggregation, thereby reducing blood clotting. They are also precursors for certain prostaglandins, which control the inflammatory response in the body.

Reported Uses: Studies have shown that Omega 3 fatty acids help reduce high blood triglyceride levels. Omega 3 may help reduce the inflammatory response in joints and other tissues.

Section Four - Food

Psyllium

Characterizing Ingredient: Psyllium husk fiber;
Reported Uses: Psyllium is bulk-forming and is used to relieve constipation. Drink plenty of water.

Rennin

Characterizing Ingredient: Lactase and Rennin.
Actions: Lactase and rennin are enzymes, which help digest milk sugar and protein.
Reported Uses: May aid in digestion of milk products.

The first step in making cheese is to separate the milk into curds and whey. Curds are milk solids that consist of casein, which is milk protein, water, fat and lactose (milk sugar). Whey is a yellowish liquid composed of lactose, whey protein and water.

There are two stages in the coagulation of milk. First the starter cultures composed of lactic acid bacteria, (among the friendly bacteria).

Following this is added the rennet, which is the clotting enzyme factor. Rennet is the dried extract of rennin. This is the enzyme that is most responsible for the clotting of milk. The traditional base of this was from an animal source, although vegetable sources may also be employed in place of the rennin. Science has also created microorganisms, similar in action.

In modern times we have forms of rennet derived from animal, vegetable or microorganisms. Animal rennet is derived from the stomach of a suckling mammal, generally a calf or lamb. This has been the traditional way to make cheese. Vegetable

Section Four - Food

rennet is derived from plants and modified to mimic the animal form. Microbial rennet is created through the process of fermentation (bacteria and fungi).

Saw Palmetto

Characterizing Ingredient: (Fatty acids and sterols)

<u>Actions:</u> Has weak anti-androgenic and anti-inflammatory effects.

Reported Uses: Widely used in Europe to support prostate health, in men over the age of 50.

Spirulina

Characterizing Ingredient: (Beta carotene: 400-1000 IU; B-12: 1 mcg; Protein: 200-400 mg per tablet)

Actions: Spirulina is an excellent vegetarian source of vitamin B-12 and also contains beta-carotene.

St. John's Wort (hypericum perforatum)

This plant has been used for centuries to treat nervous disorders, anti-viral conditions, inflammation, wound healing and depression. The latest research has focused on hypericin and pseudo-hypericin which have been found to be effective anti-depressants.

St. John's Wort contains a number of elements including, along with hypericin, flavonoids, phyto-sterols, tannins and xanthrones. Both hypericin and the xanthrones contain monoamine oxidase (MAO), which is a standard treatment for depression, as has been reported in a study published in the <u>British Medical Journal</u>. In several placebo controlled studies the number of side effects were more frequent in the non-hypericum group. Hypericin is recommended for mild depression due to it's limited side effects.

In 1994, Vorbach and others conducted a

Section Four - Food

study of 135 patients diagnosed with depression who were given either St. John's Wort or imipramine, an anti-depression drug. The trial period lasted for six weeks. The success of the therapy was determined by using the depression scales (HAMD & CGI). All tests showed slightly better in the St. John's group, and also that the adverse reactions were lower with the St. John's Wort than with the prescription drug.

Hypericum, is now licensed for use in insomnia, depression and anxiety. The few cautions are a photo-sensitivity and a hyper-sensitivity when the skin is exposed to the sun. Avoid if pregnant or nursing.

Tea Tree Oil

The tea tree (Melalenuca alternifolia), a member of the Myrtaceae family, shares its roots with the eucalyptus tree, as a native of northern New South Wales, Australia.

The essential oil of the tea tree is renowned for its antifungal and antiseptic qualities, and has enjoyed worldwide popularity since the 1980's. But, the people of its homeland have appreciated the health-giving benefits of tea tree for many centuries. Native Australians applied tea tree poultices to their wounds and skin disorders.

Australian scientists had already begun clinical testing of the antibacterial properties of tea tree as early as the 1920s. One physician, Dr. Arthur Penfold of the Sydney Museum of Applied Arts and Sciences, found that tea tree oil was at least 10 times more effective than carbolic acid (phenol), a standard antiseptic in use at the time. Penfold presented tea tree oil as a

Section Four - Food

"dependable and effective topical treatment" to the Royal Society in 1923. Private physicians and public hospitals began using the oil to sterilize instruments, and to prevent infection, in surgical patients.

Pure tea tree oil contains 48 known compounds, two of which, Terpinene-4-ol (healing), and cineole (anti-septic), are of critical importance.

The Australian Standards Association (ASA) has established certain criteria to ensure quality in the manufacturing of tea tree oil.

In one study, conducted by the Department of Podiatric Medicine and Surgery at Wilmington Hospital, Delaware, the activity of tea tree oil was evaluated against 58 clinical pathogens, including Candida, Aspergillus, Tricholphyton, Penicillium, and Epidermophyton species. Tea tree oil proved effective against all of the pathogens but a single strain of Escherichia floccosum.

Some conditions which may be treated effectively with tea tree oil are:

Rashes: including diaper rash, psoriasis, eczema, poison ivy, insect bites:
Combine 1 teaspoon of tea tree oil with 1/8 cup of cold-pressed "carrier" oil, such as avocado, apricot kernel, or sweet almond. Using a cotton ball, apply this solution directly to affected areas of the skin.
Note: This formula can also be used to speed the healing of burns & cuts.

Coughs: nasal, and bronchial congestion:
Add 10-15 drops of tea tree oil to a vaporizer.

Ringworm: athlete's foot, warts, or boils:

Section Four - Food

Apply 1-2 drops of tea tree oil undiluted directly to the affected areas.

<u>Note:</u> Do not apply the oil directly to sensitive facial skin. For areas on the face, dilute the tea tree oil with a cold-pressed oil.

<u>Dandruff:</u>

Add 7 drops of tea tree oil to a quarter-sized amount of shampoo in the palm of your hand. Using small circular motions, massage into the scalp with fingertips. Avoid contact with eyes.

Valerian

Valerian is a relaxant that may be used for anxiety, nervousness, headache, insomnia and intestinal cramps. The sedative element in valerian is valepotriates, similar to the ingredient in valium, but is milder and safer. Valerian is not affected by alcohol or barbiturates, yet it can reduce blood pressure. Large amounts can cause nausea, headache, blurred vision and restlessness.

Wheatgrass

Wheatgrass juice is a powerful cleanser and as a result may cause some nausea. Chlorophyll will bring toxins stored in the cells or in the fatty tissues into the bloodstream. Wheatgrass juice is very high in enzymes and chlorophyll, containing up to 70% chlorophyll, recognized as an important blood builder. The essential molecule of chlorophyll closely resembles the hemin molecule. This combines with protein to form hemoglobin. In fact, about the only difference is that chlorophyll contains magnesium as its' central atom, while hemin contains iron.

Section Four - Food

Wheat picks up 92 of the 102 minerals in the soil and contains all the vitamins so far isolated. One ounce of wheatgrass juice equals two pounds of produce. Chlorophyll will arrest the growth and proliferation of the unfriendly bacteria. Rapp and Gurney at Loyola University established that water soluble chlorophyll inhibits the action of proteolytic bacteria, which break proteins into simpler substances and enzymes. When wheatgrass is taken internally, whether oral or anal, it inhibits the putrefaction of protein by the bacteria commonly formed in the digestive tract of meat eaters.

Dr.Chiu-Lan Lai Ph.D. at the University of Texas System Cancer Center, Department of Biology, Houston, Texas, has determined through using the Ames Bacterial Mutagenicity Test that chlorophyll is the active factor in wheat sprout extract, which inhibits the metabolic activity of carcinogens.

In a twenty year study it was discovered that beta-carotene, a naturally occurring element in carrots and leafy green vegetables, significantly reduced the risk of lung cancer in cigarette smokers and negated the effects of 30 years.

The National Cancer Institute reports that 19 of 21 studies indicated diets high in beta-carotene contributes to at least a 40% risk reduction in developing some types of cancer.

Additives

Acidifiers - Control acidity of processed foods, make dough rise, and can change flavor and tartness. Some acidifiers are used as preservatives or anti-browning agents. These can erode teeth and cause cavities.

Agar-Agar - Seaweed extract used as thickener, or stabilizer in soft drinks, ice cream, custard, icing and jelly. May act as a laxative. Some allergic reactions.

Alginates - made from algin found in brown algae. Algin is used as a thickener, stabilizer and crystallization inhibitor.

Alkalies - are pH adjusting agents and act as preservatives and flavor enhancers.

Aluminum Hydroxide - leavener in baked goods.

Ammonium Chloride - dough conditioner, in large doses may cause nausea and upset stomach.

Ammonium Sulfate - dough conditioner

Anti-browning Agents - (sulfite compounds). Prevents cut fruits and vegetables from oxidizing and turning brown.

Anti-caking Agents - prevents powders like salt, baking powder and soft drink powders from absorbing water and becoming hard.

Anti-foaming Agents - found in fruit juices, wine, beer, jelly, milk products and baked goods. Some have been found to be poisonous in large doses.

Anti-myotic Agents - mold inhibitors found in bread, cheese, processed meats, dried fruit, syrup and jelly. (sodium nitrate & calcium propionate).

Anti-oxidants - slows the oxidation of oils and oil based products and prevents rancidity. A natural anti-oxidant is tocopherol (vitamin E). BHA and BHT are anti-oxidants. These are freshness preservers, used

Section Four - Food

to slow the oxidation of oils and oil based products, some are natural, such as vitamins C and E, many are synthetic, many are toxic.

Ascorbates - anti-oxidants used in milk and meat products and related to vitamin C.

Ascorbic Acid - natural or synthetic vitamin C, used as an anti-oxidant.

Benzoyl Peroxide - To lighten the color of flour.

BHA and BHT - (butylated hydroxyanisole, butylated hydroxytoluene) anti-oxidants used in foods such as butter, cream, shortening, bacon, powdered soup, fried foods, whipped topping, salad dressing, breakfast bars, peanut butter, canned fruits and vegetables, bottled oil, and foods containing artificial coloring and flavoring, potato chips, gelatin desserts. Accumulate in body fat and have been associated with kidney damage, allergies and birth defects.

Binders - to hold processed meats and snack foods together. Many binders are natural substances, such as various forms of calcium.

Bleaching Agents - destroy vitamin E. These are found in flour, baked goods, cheese, fats and oils.

Brominated Vegetable Oil - an emulsifier in soft drinks, ice cream & baked goods. Accumulative and linked to heart, liver, kidney, thyroid, pancreas, spleen and testicle problems.

1,3 Butylene Glycol - humectant or flavor carrier in flavored and colored foods. (drowsiness, nervousness, depression, indigestion or respiratory problems).

Calcium Carbonate - (a yeast food) alkali,

Section Four - Food

neutralizer and flavor carrier in bread, candy, ice cream, wine, baking powder and syrup.

Calcium Chloride - firming agent in canned fruit, jelly, pie filling, cheese and canned tomatoes. May cause stomach or heart problems.

Calcium Lactate - a salt of lactic acid used as an anti-browning agent and firming agent in fruits and vegetables, a buffer in soft drinks, a yeast food in bread; also used in evaporated milk.

Calcium Oxide - dough conditioner used in bread, baked goods, dairy products and candy. Associated with skin and mucous membrane problems.

Calcium Phosphate - bleaching agent and yeast food in flour and baked goods. Tri-calcium phosphate is used as an anti-caking agent in seasoned salt, table salt and vanilla powder.

Calcium Sulfate - (plaster of Paris) dough conditioner used in flour products, sherry, jelly, cottage cheese, brewed drinks and hard cheeses.

Carrageenan - made from seaweed, and is used as a stabilizer, emulsifier, thickener in milk products, chocolate, desserts, dressings, beer, pudding and gelatin desserts. may cause ulcers in infants.

Casein - milk protein, texturizer in frozen desserts.

Chlorine and Chlorine Dioxide - used as a bleaching agent in flour. Destroys vitamin E.

Citric Acid - a natural or synthetic acidifier or anti-oxidant in frozen desserts, soft drinks, canned meats, fruit juice, jelly, margarine, canned fruits and vegetables, cheese, mayonnaise, salad dressing, wine and candy. (destroys tooth enamel, causes cavities).

CMC - (carbo-methyl-cellulose) a form of cellulose from plants used as a texturizer, thickener, stabilizer, emulsifier in ice cream, candy, icing, jelly, beer, pie filling, pie crust, bread, salad dressing, whipped cream, syrup and processed cheese. May cause cancer.

Cyclamates - once used in many foods as the principal artificial sweetener, were banned several years ago after they were shown to cause birth defects and cancer. Replaced by saccharin, now associated with cancer, kidney disease, and birth defects.

Dextrin - crystallization inhibitor, anti-foaming agent in beer and candy and a flavor carrier in oils and powdered foods. This is made from starch.

Disodium Phosphate - emulsifier, binder and buffer in evaporated milk, cured meats, sauces, soft drinks, chocolate products, and has been known to irritate skin and mucous membranes.

EDTA - (Ethylenediamine tetra-acetic acid) seqeustrant and anti-oxidant in salad dressing, sandwich spreads, margarine, seafood, mayonnaise, beer, canned goods, soft drinks. Linked to skin irritations, liver and kidney damage, cramps, allergic reactions and mineral deficiencies.

Ethyl Cellulose - *see* CMC

Fumaric Acid - acidifier in gelatin desserts, pudding, jelly, candy, powdered soft drinks.

Gelatin - thickener, stabilizer or crystallization inhibitor. Made from animal protein (any animal part which can not be used in any other industry is sterilized and pulverized into animal gelatin).

Section Four - Food

Gluconates - (calcium, ferrous and sodium gluconate) flavor enhancers, sequestrants, buffers or firming agents in confections, canned fruit, candy, canned vegetables and soft drinks. made from sugar (glucose) (may cause stomach or heart problems).

Glutamates - flavor enhancers in processed foods.

Glycerin - (glycerol) humectant, flavor carrier, anti-staling agent in gelatin desserts, soft drinks, candy, baked goods and some meat products.

GMP - (disodium guanylate) very powerful flavor enhancer. This is often used with MSG and IMP in powdered soup, sauces, spreads and some canned vegetables. Can be harmful to those with gout and other uric acid based conditions.

GRAS - (Generally Recognized As Safe) It was initially formulated in 1958 as a guideline to the industry. Gradually many of those items listed were proven to be unsafe. Among these were the cyclamates, saccharin, saffrole and brominated vegetable oil. Many other GRAS additives have not been tested, although the Food and Drug Administration has been reevaluating each of the additives on the list. Food manufacturers are allowed to add chemicals they feel are safe to the list without obtaining FDA permission. Of the hundreds of chemicals now on the list in order to eliminate an item, it must first be proven to be harmful.

Hydrogen Peroxide - Dough conditioner, bleaching agent and anti-mycotic agent used in cheese, butter and baked goods.

Hydrogenated Vegetable Oil - Polyunsaturated

oil to which hydrogen has been added to keep the oil solid at higher temperatures or to prolong shelf-life...used in margarine, shortening, cooking oil, baked and fried foods, coffee creamer, imitation milk, peanut butter, These have been associated with high cholesterol levels and heart disease.

Hydrolyzed Vegetable Protein - Filler or flavor enhancer made from vegetable protein (usually soy) which has been made water-soluble...used in instant soup, hot dogs, canned meat dishes, gravy mixes, as well as in imitation meats.

IMP - (disodium inosinate) powerful flavor enhancer, often used with GMP and MSG. Related to GMP.

Iodides - Chemicals made from iodine, a " trace element" necessary for proper thyroid functioning... includes potassium and cuprous iodide and potassium and calcium iodate...used as crystallization inhibitors in salt and as dough improvers in bread...if taken in large amounts can cause a form of goiter and may cause allergic reactions.

Lactic Acid - natural or synthetic acidifier, antioxidant, antimycotic agent, or buffer in bread, cheese, olives, butter, beverages, baked goods & beer.

Lecithin - antioxidant usually made from soybeans but present in a number of foods. Emulsifier, stabilizer, thickener, crystallization inhibitor. Used in cereal, margarine, oil products, frozen desserts, chocolate, baked goods, soft drinks. May reduce cholesterol levels in arteries.

Locust Bean Gum - carob, St Johns Bread, see vegetable gum.

Section Four - Food

Magnesium - used as buffers, neutralizers, alkalies, or anti-caking agents in soft drinks, dairy products, baked goods, brewed drinks, cocoa, salt, canned vegetables, etc. Magnesium silicate may be linked to kidney damage, magnesium carbonate, can be toxic in large amounts.

Malic Acid - natural or synthetic is apple acid, acidifier in baked goods, fruit drinks, candy, butter, iced tea mix, dairy products, ice cream, etc.

Manitol - see sweeteners.

Mono/Di Glycerides - (and additives made form them) antistaling agents, dough conditioners, anti-foaming agents, crystallization inhibitors, stabilizers, baked goods, chocolate, peanut butter, whipped toppings, candy, margarine, jelly, frozen desserts.

MSG - (monosodium glutamate) Flavor enhancer made originally from soybeans, sugar, or seaweed... used in many processed foods, including soup and soup mixes, canned vegetables, processed fish, canned meat, frozen food, seasonings, salad dressings, potato chips, mayonnaise, baked goods. Allergic Reactions: (Chinese Restaurant Syndrome) are common. Has been known to cause brain damage in mice, and may not be safe for human fetuses.

Nitrates and Nitrites - (including sodium and potassium nitrate and sodium nitrite) Antimycotic agents and colors in processed meats like bacon, lunch meats, hot dogs, canned or packaged ham, sausage, etc... can be toxic in moderate amounts... linked to cancer, brain damage, arthritis, etc...labeled dangerous by FDA but not banned because of ability to prevent botulism, especially in canned hams.

Oxystearin - animal fat compound used as crystallization inhibitor in mayonnaise, sugar, salad dressing, yeast, etc.

Papain - enzyme from papaya plant...used as meat tenderizer...taken raw and in large amounts can interfere with digestion.

Paraben - (parahydroxybenzoic acid compounds) preservatives or antimycotic agents used in variety of foods, including soft drinks and beer...related to sodium benzoate.

Pectin - natural gelling agent, thickener, or emulsifier in jelly, salad dressing, barbecue sauce, yogurt, frozen desserts, cranberry sauce, syrup, soft drinks.

Phosphates - Emulsifiers, acidifiers, texturizers in evaporated milk, baked goods, soft drinks. Related to sodium phosphate and phosphoric acid.

Phosphoric Acid - acidifier in frozen desserts, brewed drinks, cheese, candy, baked goods, dairy goods, jelly, soft drinks. This is used as a sequestrant in animal fats, and can irritate in concentrated doses. Related to sodium phosphate and to phosphates.

Polysorbate - compounds of polyoxyethylene. Sorbitan, emulsifiers in baked goods, gelatin products, soup, ice cream, candy, artificial toppings, non-dairy creamer, pickles, soft drinks, spreads, chocolate. May cause diarrhea and organ damage in large doses.

Polysorbate 60 - see polysorbate.

Potassium - compounds made from potassium. Normally used as buffers, preservatives, or yeast foods in soft drinks, candy, diet jelly, brewed drinks.

Section Four - Food

Potassium Chloride - Yeast food, salt substitute, or buffer in brewed drinks, jelly, soft drinks, and some baked goods...linked to ulcers, kidney irritation, and in large doses digestive disorders.

Potassium Nitrate - see nitrites.

Propionate - (propionic acid; calcium and sodium propionate) Antimycotic agents in bread, baked goods, cheese, and chocolate, may cause allergic reactions.

Propyl Gallate - antioxidant often used with BHA and BHT in oil, soft drinks, meat products, candy, ice cream, dried soup, nuts, chewing gum, baked goods,...linked to liver damage.

Propylene Glyco l - humectant, flavor carrier, or texturizer in chocolate, soft drinks, coconut, meat products, canned icing, baked goods...also used in antifreeze.

St. Johns Bread Gum - see locust bean gum, in vegetable gums.

Salt - flavor enhancer and occasional preservative in a large number of processed foods, consumed in large amounts by most humans...linked to high blood pressure, hardening of the arteries and water retention...see sodium.

Silicon - any number of additives made from the element, silicon...includes Silica (silicon dioxide) and silicates, which are anti-caking agents in powdered foods like salt, dry soup mixes, nondairy creamer, baking goods, vanilla powder. Silicones (like dimethylpolysiloxane and methyl silicone), which are anti-foaming or anti-splattering agents in wines,

Section Four - Food

soft drinks, syrup, yeast, vegetable oil, soup, gelatin, sugar. Silicon additives combined with magnesium or sodium cause kidney problems.

Sodium - a number of major additives are based on the element, sodium, including sodium chloride (salt). It is largely the sodium which causes most of the problems people experience with salt.

Sodium Aluminum Phosphate - used with sodium bicarbonate as buffer in flour and cheese products.

Sodium Aluminum Sulfate - aluminum "salt" which forms the "SAS" in many baking powders... used in baked goods with baking powder added... has been associated with kidney failure in rats.

Sodium Benzoate - (and Benzoic Acid) preservatives and antimycotic agents, in pickles, baked goods, ice cream, mince meat, margarine, jelly, soft drinks, fruit juice, salad dressing. Can cause intestinal upset. Benzoic acid has damaged nerves and brains and stunted growth of animals.

Sodium Bicarbonate - (baking soda) leavener in large number of baked goods. Buffer in soft drinks.

Sodium Bisulfite - (and Sodium Dioxide) antioxidants, antimycotic agents, anti-browning agents in grapes and grape juice, dried fruit, powered soup, canned food, soft drinks, dehydrated potatoes, destroys Vitamin B1. May cause genetic mutations.

Sodium Carbonate - neutralizer in butter, cocoa.

How To Set Up A Natural Kitchen

Apple Corer a simple stainless steel unit for coring apples and similar fruit quickly.

Blender may be used to grind nuts, make bread

Section Four - Food

crumbs, various grain and seed flours, or puree or liquify. Essentially all that is needed is two speeds. It is important to obtain a blender that detaches the jar from the base for easy and total cleaning. These sometimes come with a smaller 8 ounce jar, which is great for grinding, seeds & nuts.

Coffee Grinder obtained in a hardware store.

Crock pot is a great time saving device, for those foods such as beans, other legumes and grains which take a longer time to prepare. With a crock pot you may prepare foods at a much lower temperature, while you are away for the day, and at the same time, preserve the safety of enzymes which are destroyed by higher temperatures (over 180 degrees Fahrenheit).

Double Boiler will keep food at an even temperature without the chance of burning it, particularly in creamed foods.

Grain mill or a good substitute is a coffee mill, and is great for grinding small seeds and grains, or for grinding smaller quantities of more common foods.

Juicer comes in a wide variety of sizes and prices. The important aspects are that the blade be stainless steel, the basket should preferably be stainless steel also, although a plastic coated one will suffice. Do not use an aluminum basket, since it can react with the acid found in some juiced items. Another important aspect to consider is the revolutions per minute of the motor. A preferred speed is about 5,000 revolutions per minute. This insures that ground pulp is spun fast enough to extract the juice properly. If the rotation of the motor is not sufficient, then the pulp will still retain

Section Four - Food

much of the juice. Another aspect is to obtain a juicer that is heavy enough not to bounce around while spinning. Often the casing is plastic, which costs less but does not supply the weight necessary to stabilize the juicer. The best type of juicer tears the flesh of the food and then squeezes out the juice through an hydraulic press, but these are quite expensive.

Knives   the essential knives are generally a paring knife, a chef or French knife, which comes with a triangular blade, and is great for chopping and slicing. A bread knife which comes with serrated teeth, and a carving knife which is also good for slicing.

Shredder there are several good machines available for shredding and slicing vegetables and fruits into various shapes. These include stringing, slicing, serrating, sticks and grating. They help in making cole slaw. Add shape and variety to vegetable salads.

Skillet is a great kitchen helper when stir cooking onions and garlic. Cast Iron maintain an even heat.

Sprouter   There are many types of sprouters available. Refer to the sprouting section in this book.

Vegetable Streamer These come in two basic varieties. One is of bamboo and the other is collapsible stainless steel, that will adjust its' size to fit any pan.

Waterless Cookware the best form of cookware, but it is extremely expensive. The reason for this is that the sides and bottom are layered in stainless steel creating a sandwich of carbon steel and aluminum. This allows for heat penetration without burning.

Wire Whisk   is an easy tool when you want to eliminate lumps combining dry and wet ingredients.

Section Four - Food

Wok the classic wok is cast iron, which works best over a gas range. Newer versions may be used over any type of heat.

Wooden Spoons & Forks in various sizes are a great help to avoid scratching the metal in pans.

Natural Sweeteners vs. Refined Sugar

When substituting honey, maple syrup, agave or stevia for refined sugar in a recipe, a few guidelines will help keep things palatable. In using honey, use one half the required amount. Maple syrup, use one third. Stevia comes in powdered and liquid forms. **Two drops** of Stevia liquid is equal to **one teaspoon** of white sugar. **One teaspoon** of Stevia is equal to **one cup** of sugar. Agave is the nectar of a cactus. Use **one half** agave to sugar. Both Stevia and agave have a low glycemic index & contain zero calories.

Nutritional & Transitional Changes:

The following changes are to be applied over the first 8 weeks of your new life style. We suggest that you implement at least one change per week and preferably two changes.

These changes are not difficult, merely challenging. Remember, if you need guidance:

www.perfecthealthnow.com

Section Four - Food

SUBTRACT	ADD
fried	steamed, raw
refined flour	whole grains, oat bran, wheat bran
refined sugars	honey, maple syrup, barley malt, agave, stevia, dried fruit
meat	grain loaves, whole grain (flourless) bread
boiled or canned veggies	steamed, baked, raw vegetables
coffee	whole grain beverages, pero, barley
pekoe tea	herbal teas
refined grains	whole grains
soy sauce (commercial)	gentle tamari, bragg liquid aminos
salt	kelp, dulse (ground), vegit, dried herbs
vinegar (commercial)	apple cider vinegar
soft drinks	fruit juice, water

Section Four - Food

Entrees

Herbs to Flavor Entrees

Anise
Basil
Bay
Caraway
Chives
Coriander
Dill Weed
Garlic
Italian Seasoning
Oregano
Parsley
Rosemary
Sage
Savory
Tarragon
Thyme

Stuffed Green Peppers

8 green peppers
2 cups brown rice (cooked)
1 tsp. Bragg Aminos or gentle tamari
1 onion (diced)
1 stalk celery (diced)
½ cup tomatoes (diced)
1 tsp. Kelp (ground)
1 cup whole grain bread crumbs

Core peppers and save seeds. Combine
next 6 ingredients and stuff peppers.
Place peppers in oiled baking dish.
Sprinkle bread crumbs over top of peppers.
Place in 375 degree oven for 30 minutes or
until tender.

Chinese Peas & Mushrooms

1 lb. Chinese peas (trimmed)
½ lb. mushrooms (sliced)
½ tsp. Bragg Aminos or gentle tamari
½ cup water

Saute Chinese peas and Bragg aminos/tamari in water for 8 minutes. Add the mushrooms and cook another 3 minutes.

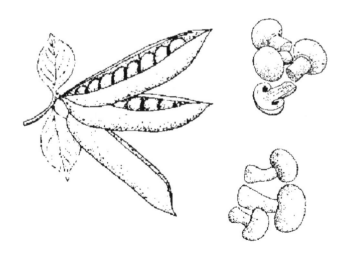

Dolmadakia

(Stuffed Grape Leaves)

1 jar grape leaves
½ cup uncooked long grain brown rice
2 cups onion (finely chopped)
2 tbs. Parsley (finely chopped)
2 tbs. mint leaves (finely chopped)
2 tsp. dill weed

Place grape leaves in a pan of warm water to separate them and draw off the brine. Lay leaves on paper towel. Combine remaining ingredients. Place 1 rounded tsp. or tbs. (Depending on size of leaves) per leaf, vein side up and stem toward you. Fold over sides and roll leaf up. Layer stuffed grape leaves in a 3 qt. Saucepan, side by side and close together. Place a heat resistant plate on top to press. Pour enough boiling water to cover leaves, and simmer for 1 1/2 hours. Serve cool.

Mint

Tofu Stew

½ lb. tofu (diced)
2 onions (sliced)
2 cloves garlic (minced)
2 stalks celery (diced)
2 tbs. oil (soy or safflower)
2 potatoes (diced)
2 cups yams (diced
1 tomato (diced)
2 tsp. Bragg Aminos or gentle tamari
1 bay leaf
1 1/2 tsp. Basil
½ tsp. cinnamon
5 cups purified water

Saute tofu, onion, garlic, celery and basil in oil for 5 minutes. Combine with remaining ingredients in large saucepan, on low to medium heat until the potatoes are tender.

Vegetable Rice Tofu

1 onion sliced
½ lb. Mushrooms (sliced)
½ lb. Kale (small pieces)
1 cup mung bean sprouts
1 lb. Firm tofu (cubed)
2 tbs. Bragg Aminos or gentle tamari
4 cups brown rice (cooked)

Saute onion in ¼ cup of water 10 minutes. Add tofu and mushrooms. Cook another ten minutes. Add kale, bean sprouts and Bragg Aminos. Cover and steam 5 minutes to wilt kale. Mix in brown rice. Then serve.

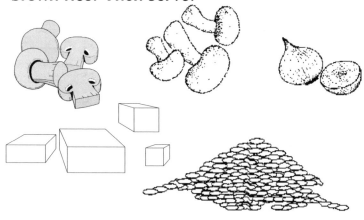

Cauliflower Rice Casserole

2 cups long grain brown rice (soak 6 hours)
4 cups hot water
1 potato medium size - diced)
1 small cauliflower bunch (into flowerettes)
2 tbs. soy or canola oil
¼ tsp. caraway seeds
¼ tsp. allspice (ground
¼ tsp. ginger (ground)
¼ tsp. parsley flakes
¼ tsp. mustard seed
1 tsp. Bragg Aminos or gentle tamari

Saute caraway and mustard see in oil. Add rice,
cauliflower and potato and saute 1 minute more.
Add water and remaining ingredients and cook over
medium heat, stirring occasionally. Let stand
20 minutes.

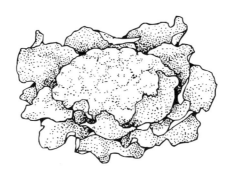

Meat Free Balls

1 cup walnuts
2 cloves garlic
1 onion
1 carrot
1 stalk celery
2 sprigs parsley
2 tbs. poultry seasoning
2 tsp. Bragg Aminos or gentle tamari
½ cup rolled oats
2 tbs. arrowroot powder
3 tbs. soy or canola oil
1 cup tomato juice

Grind first 7 ingredients together. Add aminos
or tamari, rolled oats and arrowroot powder,
using sufficient tomato juice to bind. Shape into
small balls or patties and set touching each other
in an oiled baking pan. Bake in 375 to 400 degree
oven until browned, basting occasionally with juice.

Grain Burgers

½ cup walnuts (ground)
1 cup rolled oats
2 tbs. Arrowroot powder
1 onion (small - minced)
½ tsp. sage
1 tsp. Bragg Aminos or gentle tamari
1 clove garlic (minced)
2 tbs. Soy oil
2/3 cup tomato juice

Combine the first 7 ingredients with 3 tbs. of the tomato juice. Form into patties and place in oiled baking dish. Bake at 375 degrees until browned. Add remaining juice and simmer until juice is evaporated. Serve on whole grain buns with lettuce and tomato slice.

Lentil Rice Casserole

1 ¼ cups lentils (pureed) or cooked beans
1 1/2 cups brown rice (cooked)
4 tomatoes (diced)
1 tbs. Italian seasoning
2 tbs. arrowroot powder
1 onion (small - minced)
¼ cup chives
½ tsp. rosemary
½ cup soy milk
3 tbs. soy oil

Combine first 8 ingredients, mixing well. Fold in soy milk and oil and bake in oiled baking dish in a 275 degree oven until the top is browned.

Vegetarian Loaf

1 1/2 cups peas (soaked 6 hours)
1 1/2 cups beans (soaked 12 hours)
1 1/2 cups brown rice (soaked 12 hours)
3 tbs. Soy oil
6 tomatoes (diced)
1 onion (small - diced)
2 cloves garlic (minced)
¼ tsp. Italian seasoning
3 tsp. Arrowroot powder
1 cup tomato juice
2 tbs. Bragg Aminos or gentle tamari

Run the grain and beans through a grinder. Add in next 6 ingredients. Form into a loaf in oiled baking dish. Bake in 325 degree oven for 45 minutes, basting with tomato juice and aminos periodically. Serve with tomato sauce or rolled oat gravy.

Fettuchine Italiano

1 lb. Whole wheat fettuchine
4 quarts purified or distilled water
2 tbs. Soy oil
1 clove garlic (minced)
1 onion (diced)

Bring water to a rolling boil. Add 1 tbs of oil. Drop
in fettuchine a little at a time, so as not to break the
boil. If the water begins to boil over, lower the heat.
Once the fettuchine is in the pan, lower the heat to
a point where the fettuchine is still rolling. Cook 6 to 7
minutes, until tender. If overcooked, the pasta will fall
apart. Saute the garlic and onion in the remaining oil.
Add to the pasta. Serve with <u>Meat Free Balls</u> and some
<u>Tomato Sauce</u>, or garlic and flax seed oil.

Tostada

1 package Organic Corn Tortillas
  mixed bean sprouts
1 bunch red leaf <u>or</u> romaine (sliced thin)
1 avocado (sliced)
1 tomato (diced)
1 onion (diced)
1 cup Tomato Sauce (recipe under SAUCES)

Place a tortilla on a lightly oiled skillet, turning several times until quite warm. Cover ½ of tortilla with a layer of sprouts. Follow with layers of lettuce, avocado, tomato, onion and any other raw greens available. Top with Tomato Sauce, fold and eat.

Mint

Sauces

Herbs to Flavor Sauces

Anise
Basil
Bay
Celery
Chives
Dill Weed
Garlic
Italian Seasoning
Onion
Oregano
Mint
Parsley
Rosemary
Sage
Savory
Thyme

Eggplant Tomato Sauce

8 cups eggplant (diced)
1 cup diced onion
1 cup diced celery
2 cups diced tomatoes
¼ cup apple cider vinegar
1 clove garlic (minced)
1 tsp. Honey

Saute the eggplant, onion, garlic and celery in an oiled skillet. Stir to prevent sticking. Add tomatoes, vinegar and honey. Simmer 20 minutes, stirring occasionally.

Catsup

6 oz. Tomato paste (or crushed tomatoes)
1/8 cup apple cider vinegar
1/3 cup apple juice
1 tsp. Honey
1 tsp. Bragg Aminos or gentle tamari
½ tsp. Oregano
1/8 tsp. Dry mustard
¼ tsp. Garlic powder

Mix tomatoes, vinegar and apple juice in a jar. Add honey, aminos or tamari and herbs. Shake well. If tomatoes are used, add 1 tsp. Of arrowroot, heated and diluted in a little warm water. This will keep 10 days to 2 weeks.

Soy Spread

(Soy "butter")

1 cup soy milk (cold)
1 quart corn, soy or safflower oil

Place soy milk in a blender at slow speed. Very slowly add oil, until mixture becomes thick. Refrigerate this and do not make too far in advance. This has no preservatives and will not last long.

Safflower
Oil

Vanilla Sauce

1 cup soy milk (cold)
1 quart corn, soy or safflower oil
barley malt or honey
pure vanilla flavor

Place soy milk in a blender at slow speed. Very slowly add oil, until mixture becomes creamy. Add sweetener and vanilla to taste. May be used as a dessert topping. Refrigerate this and do not make too far in advance. This has no preservatives and will not last long.

Tomato Sauce 1

3 cups tomatoes
½ cup onion (diced)
½ cup green pepper (diced)
2 stalks celery (diced)
1 tbs. Soy oil
1 tbs. Honey
1 tsp. Bragg Aminos or gentle tamari
1 tsp. Sweet basil
1 garlic clove (minced)

Saute garlic and onions. Add remaining ingredients, and simmer over low heat until entire mixture thickens.

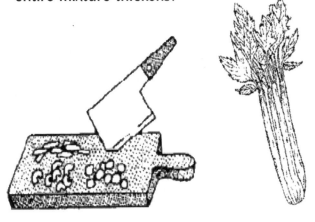

Tomato Sauce 2

8 tomatoes
1 tbs. Apple cider vinegar
2 tbs. Bragg Aminos or gentle tamari
2 tbs. soy or canola oil
1 cup purified water
1 onion (small - minced)
1 green pepper (small - diced)
1 bay leaf

Combine all ingredients in a saucepan, and simmer for 30 minutes, stirring occasionally.

Dill

Salads

Mint

Herbs to Flavor
Salads

Anise
Basil
Celery
Chives
Coriander
Dill Weed
Garlic
Italian Seasoning
Oregano
Mint
Parsley
Rosemary
Sage
Savory
Tarragon
Thyme

Mixed Sprout Salad

½ cup alfalfa sprouts
½ cup mixed bean (lentil/pea/chick)
½ cup sunflower sprouts
½ carrot (grated)
½ cucumber (sliced)
1 sprig scallion
2-3 leaves red leaf lettuce (torn small)

Toss sprouts, carrot and cucumber and serve on lettuce leaves with dressing of choice.

Apple-Cabbage-Celery

¼ head cabbage (chopped)
1 apple (diced)
2 celery stalks (cut in slices)
2 scallion stalks <u>or</u> ½ red onion (diced)
2 leaves red leaf <u>or</u> Romaine lettuce

Combine all ingredients on lettuce,
and use lemon juice with Bragg Aminos
and olive oil for dressing.

Watercress-Sprout Salad

1 cup sunflower sprouts
1 small bunch watercress (chopped)
½ cucumber (diced)
1 celery stalk (diced)
½ avaocado (diced)
1 tbs. Lemon juice (fresh squeezed)
1 or 2 leaves red leaf lettuce

Toss all ingredients lightly, and serve on a leaf of red leaf lettuce.

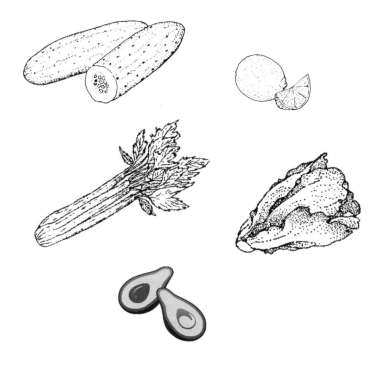

Carrot-Apple-Cabbage

½ head cabbage
3 carrots
1 apple (chopped)

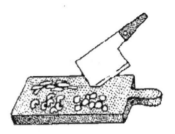

Grate cabbage and carrots and add chopped apple. Cover with tofu lemon dressing.

Sea Salad

1 cup lentil, pea & mung sprouts
¼ cup kelp <u>or</u> dulse (torn small)
½ tomato (sliced)
¼ cup scallions (diced)
1 stalk celery (chopped)
¼-½ avocado (diced)
½ lemon (juice & pulp) Mung
1 tsp. Bragg Aminos <u>or</u> gentle tamari

Combine first 6 ingredients in a bowl.
Combine lemon and Bragg Aminos <u>or</u>
tamari, and pour over the top.

Apple-Orange-Cabbage

2 apples
2 carrots
1 orange
1 level tsp. Dill weed (dried)
2 leaves of red leaf or romaine lettuce

Dice apples, grate carrots, and place on lettuce. Squeeze juice of orange over the top, and sprinkle on dill weed.

Dill

Guacamole

2 avocados
1 tsp. Lemon juice
2 cloves garlic
½ onion (diced)
2 scallions (diced)
1 tomato (diced)

Pit and mash the avocados.
Mince the garlic cloves and
add to the lemon juice, onions,
scallions and tomato. Fold together.
Makes a great dip.

Nori-Sprout Roll

2 cups alfalfa sprouts
1 cup mung bean sprouts
1 tomato (diced)
½ avocado (diced)
1 tsp. Bragg aminos or gentle tamari
6 nori sheets (cut in ½ sheets)

Combine the first 5 ingredients in a bowl, and then layer the combo onto ½ sheets of nori, and roll tightly. If you wet the seaweed lightly first, it will hold the mix together better.

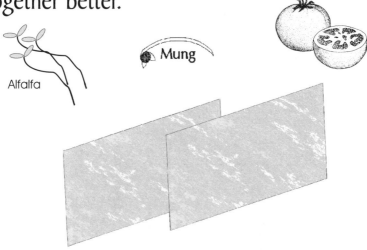

Alfalfa

Mung

Dressings

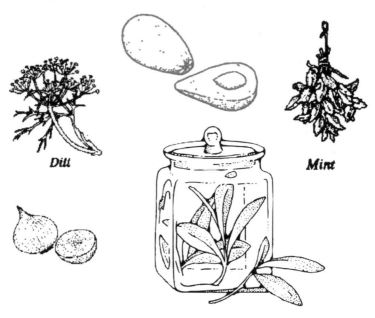

Dill

Mint

Herbs to Flavor
Dressings

Anise
Basil
Celery
Chives
Dill Weed
Garlic
Italian Seasoning
Mint
Oregano
Parsley
Poppy Seed
Rosemary
Sage
Savory
Sesame Seed
Tarragon
Thyme

Tofu Salad Dressing
(Tofu Mayo)

1 lb. Tofu (soft)
2 cloves garlic
2 tsp. lemon juice
3 tsp. Bragg Aminos or gentle tamari
2-3 oz. almond milk

Place all ingredients in a blender, and blend slowly adding the almond milk until proper consistency is reached. Blend until smooth.

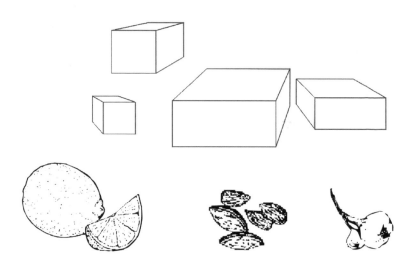

Lemon Seed Dressing

½ cup sunflower seeds (soaked 6 hours)
¼ cup purified <u>or</u> distilled water
2 tbs. lemon juice
½ tsp. raw honey, maple syrup <u>or</u>
2 drops of stevia <u>or</u> agave

Combine all ingredients in a blender
and whip until smooth.

Italian Parsley Dressing

½ cup sunflower seeds (soaked 6 hours)
¼ cup parsley
2 petals of a garlic clove (peeled)
1 cup distilled <u>or</u> purified water
2 tsp. lemon juice
1 tsp. Bragg Aminos <u>or</u> gentle tamari

Combine all ingredients in a blender
and whip until smooth.

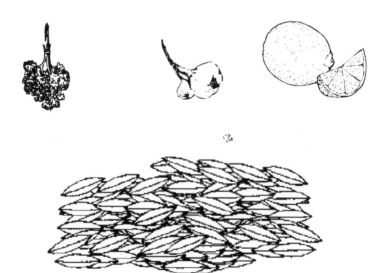

Green Goddess Dressing

¼ cup spinach

1 tomato (medium sized - diced)

½ avocado (chunked)

1 scallion

1 cup distilled <u>or</u> purified water

1 tsp. Braggs Aminos <u>or</u> gentle tamari

Combine all ingredients in a blender and combine until smooth.

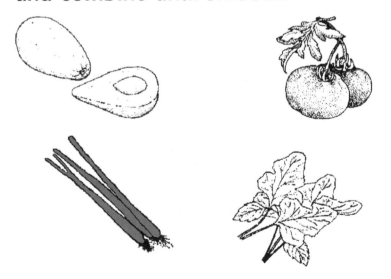

Veggie Dressing

5 tomatoes

1/8 cup lemon juice

1 tsp. Vegit

1 bunch parsley

1 tsp. Basil

½ tsp. Majoram

3 green onions

1 clove garlic

Mix ingredients in a blender. Store in refrigerator.

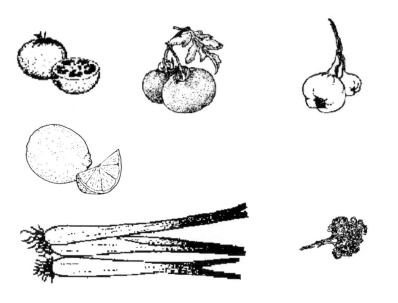

Green Herb Dressing

¼ cup chopped mint
¼ cup parsley flakes
1 tsp. chopped chives
½ tsp. dill weed
1 clove garlic (cut in ¼ pieces)
2 tsp. Bragg Aminos or gentle tamari
1 cup apple juice or tomato juice

Pour juice and Aminos in jar. Add herbs.
Shake.

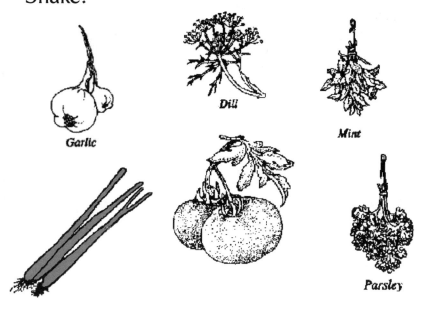

Garlic

Dill

Mint

Parsley

SAGE

Soups

Dill

Mint

Herbs to Flavor Soups

Anise
Basil
Bay
Caraway
Chives
Coriander
Dill Weed
Garlic
Italian Seasoning
Oregano
Parsley
Rosemary
Sage
Savory
Tarragon
Thyme

Barley Soup

8 cups water
¾ cup barley
2 tsp. Dill weed
1 onion (minced)
½ lb. Mushrooms (sliced)
1 bay leaf

Place barley, water, onions and herbs
in a large pot. Cover and simmer for about
2 hours. During the last 15 minutes add
the mushrooms.

Pea Soup

½ lb. Split peas
8 cups purified water or veggie juice
2 tsp. Oil (soy or safflower)
 potatoes (chunked)
½ tsp. Oregano
½ tsp. Dill weed

Soak peas for 30 minutes. Add oil to peas and water and simmer for 20 minutes. Add remaining ingredients and simmer for 30 minutes more. If you prefer "creamed" soup, run through a blender for 30 seconds.

Tomato Rice Soup

2 cups brown rice

4 cups purified water

4 tsp. Oil (soy or safflower)

¼ onion (chopped)

1 clove garlic (minced)

6 cups tomato juice

¼ tsp. Basil

Combine brown rice, water and oil in large saucepan. Bring to a boil, stirring occasionally. Set heat on low and simmer, 45 minutes. Add onion and garlic, tomato juice and basil, and simmer for another 15 minutes.

Bean & Barley Soup

1 cup aduki or kidney beans (soak 8 hours)
1 cup barley (soak with the beans)
2 potatoes (diced)
1 yam (small chunks)
3 carrots (thinly sliced)
2 large onions (diced)
½ lb. Mushrooms (quartered)
2 cloves garlic (minced)
4 tomatoes (chopped)
3 tsp. Bragg Aminos or gentle tamari
1 oz. Soy or safflower oil
1 tbs. Italian seasoning
2½ cups tomato juice
5 cups purified water

Cook beans in saucepan for 1 hour using
1 tbs. Oil and enough water to equal twice
the height of the beans. Saute on medium
heat, onion, garlic, mushrooms and Italian
seasoning, in a little of the oil, stirring until
tender. Add barley, carrots, potatoes, yams,
tomatoes and juice. Cook for 30 minutes.

Rice & Pea Soup

2 ½ cups black eyed peas
6 cups water
1 large onion (chopped)
½ cup raw brown rice
2 cloves garlic (pressed)
1 bay leaf
2 tsp. Majoram
1 tbs. Bragg Aminos or gentle tamari

Place all ingredients in a large pan.
Bring to a boil and reduce heat. Cover and
simmer for 45 minutes. Remove bay leaf
and serve.

Sunflower Seed Soup

1 cup carrots (grated)
1 onion (large diced)
2 tbs. soy or canola oil
1 ½ cups water
3 tomatoes (medium/run through blender)
½ cup sunflower seed meal (use nut mill)
1 bayleaf
1 tbs. Bragg Aminos or gentle tamari
1 tbs. honey

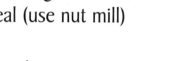

Saute carrots and onions over low heat for 3 minutes. Add water and cook until vegetables are tender. Combine with tomatoes in blender until smooth. Place back in saucepan and add remaining ingredients. Simmer 10 minutes. Serve.

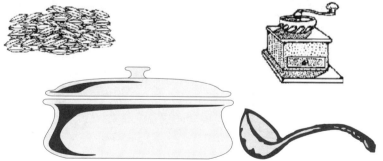

Grains

Herbs to Flavor Grains

Anise
Basil
Barley Malt
Caraway
Celery
Chives
Garlic
Honey
Italian Seasoning
Onion
Oregano
Maple Syrup
Mint
Poppy Seed
Sage
Savory

Bran Muffin

1 ¼ cups brown rice flour
½ tsp. Honey or barley malt
½ cup raisins
1 ½ cups bran
1 ¼ cups apple juice
3 tsp. Apple sauce

Combine apple juice and applesauce with honey. Add brown rice flour. Stir in bran. Add in raisins. Fold gently. Spoon into oiled muffin tin to about 2/3 full. Let rise for about 30 minutes. Bake in 350 degree oven 25 minutes.

Buckwheat Pancakes

1 cup buckwheat flour
1 cup brown rice flour
½ tsp. Cinnamon
½ tsp. Nutmeg
2½ cups apple juice

Mix dry ingredients together. Add juice and mix well. Cook on a hot griddle. Flip when holes form on top. Top with maple syrup. Makes 8-10 small pancakes.

Barley Muffin

2 cups barley flour
¼ cup honey or maple syrup
2 cups soy or almond milk
2 tbs. applesauce
½ tsp. vanilla
½ tsp. cinnamon
¼ tsp. allspice
¼ tsp. nutmeg
¼ tsp. Ginger

Combine dry ingredients. Combine wet ingredients. Fold both mixtures together. Spoon into an oiled muffin tin to a level top and bake in a 350 degree oven 30 minutes.

Rice Bread

2 cups brown rice flour
2 tsp. Honey or barley malt
1 ¼ cups apple juice or water

Mix together honey and juice. Add the honey/juice mixture to the flour. Transfer to baking dish and bake at 300 degrees for 40 minutes. Loaf is done when toothpick inserted in the center of loaf comes out clean.

Oat Corn Cakes

1 cup oat flour
½ cup corn meal
½ cup brown rice flour
1 ½ cups apple juice
2 tsp. Honey or barley malt
1 tsp. Applesauce

Combine all ingredients. Cook on a lightly oiled griddle. When top bubbles and/or edges look dry, time to flip.

Barley-Oat Waffles

3 cups apple juice
2 cups rolled oats
1 cup barley flour
½ cup brown rice flour
1 tbs. Barley malt

Combine in blender. Blend all ingredients until smooth. Allow to sit for 12-15 minutes. Ladle onto preheated waffle iron about one cup per four section waffle. (To make rice flour, ground brown rice in a coffee/nut grinder to equal ½ cup when finished.)

Desserts

Herbs to Flavor

Desserts

Allspice
Anise
Apple Concentrate
Apple Juice
Barley Malt
Cinnamon
Clove
Dates
Honey
Maple Syrup
Mint
Nutmeg
Poppy Seed
Rice Syrup
Sesame Seed
Yinnie Syrup

Frozen Banana Ice Cream

6-8 bananas (ripe/skinned/frozen)
4 oz. Honey or maple syrup
2 oz. Walnuts (shelled/crushed)

When freezing bananas, place in a zip lock bag. Best to choose bananas with freckles. Drop pieces into blender at slow speed or run through a Champion Juicer. Pour on 1 tsp. Of maple syrup per scoop. Serve with vanilla sauce topping and walnuts.

Carrot Cake

1 cup pitted dates
1 cup raisins
3½ cups carrots (raw/grated)
½ cup honey or maple syrup
½ cup cold pressed oil
1 cup walnuts

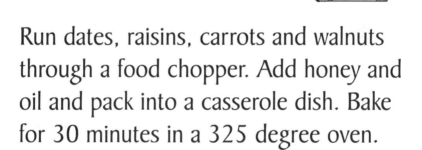

Run dates, raisins, carrots and walnuts through a food chopper. Add honey and oil and pack into a casserole dish. Bake for 30 minutes in a 325 degree oven. Top with vanilla sauce.

Carob Pudding

4 cups soy "cream"

1 cup carob powder

2 cup honey or barley malt (room temp.)

2 tbs. Pure vanilla extract

4 tsp. Arrowroot powder

Stir arrowroot in a little water to dissolve it. Slowly combine carob powder with the soy "cream" and arrowroot in a double boiler, or in a glass or stainless steel saucepan, stirring constantly to prevent sticking. Slowly add sweetener and vanilla extract, and cook until desired consistency is obtained. Cool before serving.

Carob Frosting

2 cups "natural butter" (cold)
1 cup carob powder
1 cup honey or barley malt (room temp.)
1 tbs. Pure vanilla extract
1 tsp. Pure peppermint oil

Slowly combine carob powder with the
"natural butter" until frosting consistency
is obtained. Blend in honey or barley malt
to desired sweetness. Blend in vanilla and
oil of peppermint. Refrigerate before spreading.

Apple-Corn Cake

2 cups corn meal
1 cup brown rice flour
2 grated apples
2 cups apple juice
2 tsp. Barley malt <u>or</u> honey
2 tbs. apple sauce
1 ½ tsp. Cinnamon

Combine dry ingredients. Combine wet ingredients. Combine both sets of ingredients. Cook with a watchful eye. Corn tends to stick easily. Top with vanilla sauce.

Brown Betty

2 cups slivered almond or chopped walnuts
4 cups chopped or sliced apples
1 cup honey
1 ¼ cups seedless raisins
1 tbs. Lemon juice

Create two layers of raisins, nuts and apples in that order, in a 2 quart glass baking dish. Add honey and lemon juice. Bake at 325 degrees for 45 minutes. Serve with vanilla sauce.

Rice Pudding

2 cups brown rice (cooked)
8 cups soy milk (½ gallon)
1 cup honey or barley malt
1-2 cups seedless raisins (to preference)
1 tsp. Pure vanilla extract

Combine all ingredients in a 4 quart glass baking dish. Bake at 275 degrees until mixture thickens. Serve Apple-Mint Sauce.

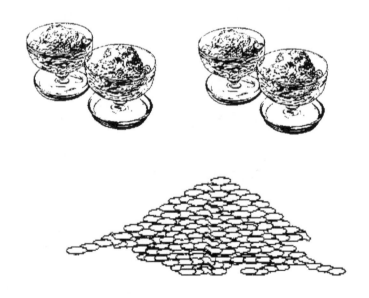

Apple-Strawberry Kanten

½ gallon unfiltered apple juice
4 tbs. Kanten or agar-agar
2 tbs. Pure vanilla extract
1 cup strawberries (cleaned & split)
4 cherries

Warm apple juice, gradually stirring in the kanten. Stir in the vanilla extract and then pour in a baking dish or mold. When cool, add strawberries, and place in refrigerator until gelled. Remove gelatin by setting mold in a pan of warm water for a few minutes. Place serving dish on top of the gelatin and turn the mold upside down. Garnish with apple slices and cherries.

Pumpkin Pudding Pie

2 tbs. Agar-agar (powdered)
1½ cups soy <u>or</u> rice milk
1 6 oz. Pumpkin (par cooked/raw)
4 oz. Honey/2 oz. Maple syrup
1 tsp. Cinnamon (ground)
½ tsp. Ginger (ground)
¼ tsp. Cloves (ground)
2 whole grain pie crusts

Bake crusts 20 minutes
in 350 degree oven.
Dissolve agar-agar in ½
cup warm soy <u>or</u> rice milk.
Combine with remaining ingredients
in order given. Pour into pie crusts
or oiled baking dish. Bake another
45-50 minutes or until knife comes
out clean. Cool until agar solidifies.
Deep dish pies will make one pie.

Baked Apple

4 Delicious apples (cored)
1 cup slivered almond or chopped walnuts
1 cup seedless raisins
2 tbs. Lemon juice

Fill apples with raisins and nuts. Sprinkle on lemon juice and bake in a glass baking dish. Bake at 350 degrees for 45 minutes. Sprinkle on cinnamon, ground clove and nutmeg, 10 minutes before done. Serve with vanilla-almond sauce.

Date Topping

½ lb. Pitted dates

Cover dates with purified or distilled water overnight. Place dates in water in a blender. Blend into syrup consistency.

Stuffed Dates/Figs

1 lb. Dates and/or Black Mission figs
1 lb. Raw or blanched almonds or pecans
½ lb. Grated coconut (unsweetened)
1 cup honey (room temperature)

Score dates or figs lengthwise and remove date pits and caps and fig stems. Insert nut meats, dip in honey layered dish, and then roll in grated coconut. Lay on waxed or brown paper and refrigerate 10-15 minutes.

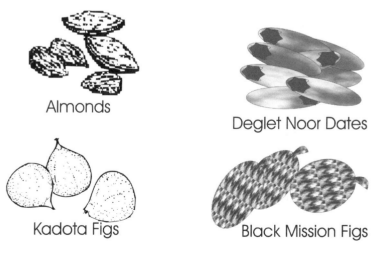

Almonds

Deglet Noor Dates

Kadota Figs

Black Mission Figs

Beverages

Herbs to Flavor

Beverages

Allspice
Apple Concentrate
Apple Juice
Anise
Barley Malt
Cinnamon
Cloves
Date Sugar
Fennel
Honey
Maple Syrup
Mint
Nutmeg
Rice Syrup
Yinnie Syrup

Smoothie
(Apple-Strawberry-Banana)

1 ½ quarts apple juice (fresh or frozen)
2 bananas (fresh or frozen)
1 ½ cups strawberries (fresh or frozen)

Place apple juice in a blender, add banana pieces, and strawberries to the top of the blender jar. Whip for 20 seconds. Serves 3-4.

Almond Milk

½ cup blanched almonds (soaked)
½ cup pine nuts (soaked)
4 cups purified or distilled water

Combine all ingredients in a blender and whip until smooth. You may substitute 4 tbs. Of raw organic almond butter for the whole almonds.

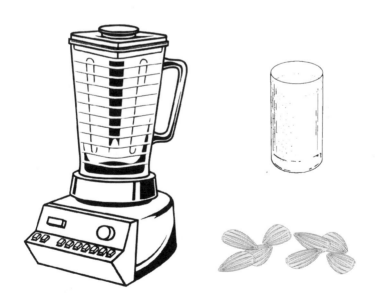

Pineapple Mint Julep

4 sprigs mint (fresh or dried)
1 lemon (juiced)
2½ cups pineapple juice (unsweetened)

Bruise the washed mint leaves with a
spoon. Add the lemon juice and let
stand for 15 minutes. Add pineapple
juice. Pour over ice in tall glasses.
Sweeten with maple syrup or honey to taste.

Mint

Fresh Fruit Cooler

¼ cup honey

3 cups water

2 cups grape juice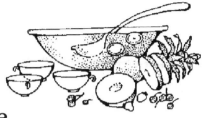

2 cups orange juice

2 cups pineapple juice

1 cup lemon juice

Preferably use fresh squeezed juice. Heat the water. Make a syrup of the and water. Let it cool. Add the grape, orange and lemon juice. Pour over ice in a pitcher. If possible use only fruit juice.

Carob Milk

4 cups almond or soy milk
2 tbs. Honey or maple syrup
2 tbs. Carob powder

Place all ingredients in a blender
and whip until smooth.

Spiced Mint

3 ½ cups of purified or distilled water
¼ tsp. Cinnamon (ground)
¼ tsp. Allspice (ground)
¼ tsp. Clove (ground)
3 mint tea bags (peppermint or spearmint)
2 oranges (juiced)
1 lemon (juiced)

Bring water to a boil. Shut off the heat. Let tea bags steep for 5 minutes. Remove bags. Add spices for 5 minutes. Strain and add fruit juice. Sweeten to taste with maple syrup or honey. Chill before serving.

Oat Milk

1 cup whole oats
5 cups water (purified or distilled)
1 tsp. Vanilla

Combine all ingredients in a saucepan.
Bring to a boil and simmer until mixture
becomes thickened. Strain and refrigerate.

Section Six - Rejuvenation Exercises

Over the years your authors have been researching every known aspect of natural healing. Of the many systems of exercise and physical enhancement commonly available, many in the long run are not technically safe for the average human structure. For example, some physical activities are one sided such as pitching a ball, while others may place too much stress at one or several of the joints such as running on a concrete surface or hardwood flooring, as they do in basketball. Some will overwork the low back or shoulder joints, while others just do not create the necessary free flowing movement at every area of the body.

9 Basics of Conditioning

Through the process of elimination we have come to the conclusion that over the long haul of several years activity, the most profound approach to maintaining a healthy body is the practice of slow, rhythmic movements which gently contract and extend the soft tissues of the body in an alternating pattern. Such an approach must also work every region of the human structure including the upper, lower, anterior, posterior, lateral and medial areas of the body. In accomplishing this there are several aspects to be encountered in order to develop the body in a total and balanced way. These we call the Basics of Conditioning. Each one of these Basics is an integral piece of developing total health.

If the guidelines presented throughout the previous sections of this book have been adhered to, the density of the tissues which leads to aging, will lessen to the point, where within a very short period of time, your body will become more flexible. Flexibility is the first of the Basics of Conditioning.

By structure and hormonal balance, most women will have a naturally limber physical structure. By the same token, most men will not. In order to develop a well-balanced program, you must define where your weaknesses among the 9 Basics of Conditioning lie, then turn each of your weaknesses into strengths.

By definition, the *9 Basics of Conditioning* are:

Section Six - Rejuvenation Exercises

flexibility - the ability to rhythmically extend the muscles (and other soft tissues) of the body.

contractility - to compress the muscles (and other soft tissues) of the body. Contractility = power.

balance - the fine point between two points of imbalance, forward/backward or right/left.

coordination - the simultaneous control between one specific body part and another.

agility - simultaneous control of the entire body.

endurance - length of time you can sustain a task.

energy - amount of "go" put into a given time.

stamina - the combination of endurance and energy.

control - there are three aspects of control.

The first is:

> *basic control* the balance between extensibility (or flexibility) and contractility (or power).

The second level is:

> *general body control* to demonstrate basic control on every area of the body, anterior, posterior, medial and lateral and from every angle, inverted as well as standing, sitting or lying down.

Section Six - Rejuvenation Exercises

The third level is:

complete control is to demonstrate general body control on a physical, mental and emotional level. In other words, complete control would encompass having emotional and mental balance as well as physical balance; mental and emotional flexibility as well as physical; emotional and mental energy as well as physical vigor. This is the only way that we can create balance in our lives.

As you progress with the programs we have presented earlier, not only will your vitality increase, but you will be lowering the density of your bodily tissues, and by combining the following physical principles you will be able, in contracting the internal and external muscles of your body, to squeeze the accumulated substances from the tissue level back into the bloodstream, to be eliminated through the organs of elimination.

Once this is accomplished, you will begin to feel and act younger on a daily basis, with occasional valleys and bumps, and a progressive energy rise.

There are a few more definitions to be included

Section Six - Rejuvenation Exercises

for a finer understanding of how the body works within this particular system. Athletes of various levels can have different manifestations of say endurance. A **dancer** has one level of endurance. A **track runner** or **basketball player** will have a different plane of endurance, and an **Olympic wrestler** will demonstrate an entirely different plateau. Yet all of these possess endurance.

Some distance athletes may be able to exert themselves over a very long stretch by nature, and even improve their ability to sustain this through practice. Yet these same people may not be able to express their exertion in the form of an energetic burst. On the opposite side of the coin, some athletes may be able to exude a burst of energy, but may not be able to continue this for more than a five or ten minute stretch.

In other words, some have endurance, while others have energy. Either of these aspects of conditioning may be improved through changes in diet and the forms of exercise employed, but when we encounter one who has both aspects, that is, energy and endurance, that combination we term stamina. Again, one athlete may be able to express their prowess through contractility which is the same thing as power. To combine **stamina** and **power** is called within this system, **strength**.

It is an easy thing to activate the energies of the body. This may be accomplished with drugs, vitamins, fasting, change of environment, breathing rhythms

Section Six - Rejuvenation Exercises

and even through encountering one who exudes this power at a level and rate of vibration that is conducive to our own. In whatever way this is accomplished, in order to sustain such a level of energy, we must have a strong, clear channel through which the energy can flow, as well as the ability to control the flow.

Often when individuals activate this energy, because their own organism is not strong enough to sustain the high rate of vibration throughout the body, problems of a physical, mental or emotional nature may arise, resulting in imbalances on any one or a combination of these aspects of our nature.

Asana & Karana Kriya

Every system of physical conditioning and control must have both isometric and isotonic aspects in order to be a complete system. Isometric exercise involves resistance or non-resistance exercises without movement. That is, you attain a position and hold it.

The most ancient organized exercise system is yoga. The non-movement aspect is called asana in the Sanskrit language. This is what is generally experienced when one practices yoga. Yet the Isotonic or movement aspect of yoga seems to be missing from the awareness of most people who practice yoga.

The following section will explore both the movement and non-movement aspects of this unique form of physical, mental, emotional and spiritual conditioning. As we penetrate into this practically unknown aspect of ancient conditioning, the *karana kriya* exercises will be pointed out.

Section Six - Rejuvenation Exercises

Some suggested websites:

www.**bragg**.com (Patricia Bragg)

www.**naturesfirstlaw**.com (David Wolfe)

www.**essenegarden**.com
(Shawn Miller & David Carmos)

www.**yogathemastermoves**.com
(Shawn Miller & David Carmos)

www.**herbsfirst**.com

www.**herbs**.org

www.**herbscancure**.com

www.**perfecthealthnow**.com (Shawn & David)

www.**viktoras**.org (Viktoras Kulvinskas)

www.**havethebestdayever**.com (David Wolfe)

Section Six - Rejuvenation Exercises

The authors with long time friend Patricia Bragg, at her home in Santa Barbara Ca. in 1998.

David and Shawn with health guru Jack LaLanne at 85 years young at his California home in 1998.

Section Six - Rejuvenation Exercises

Face & Neck

platysma stretch
(matsyasana)

Placing the chin on the chest, stretching the wide band of muscle which stretches across the front of the neck, and from the chin to the collarbone. It is best to use a mirror when first attempting this movement until the action is felt.

This band, called the platysma (pla-tis-ma), will show vertical strands when it is properly contracted.

Place the hands, fingertips spread apart, just below the collarbone. Push the fingertips in and down as you raise the chin, judging the two stretches, so that jsut as the highest point is reached with the chin, the lowest is attained with the hands.

Retain this stretch turning the chin to the right, resisting with the left hand. relax the left hand pressure, turning the chin to the center and resist with both hands. Relax the hand resistance again, and turn the chin to the left resiting with the right hand. Relax the right hand pressure, turning the chin to the center and resist with both hands, as the chin is lowerd to the chest.

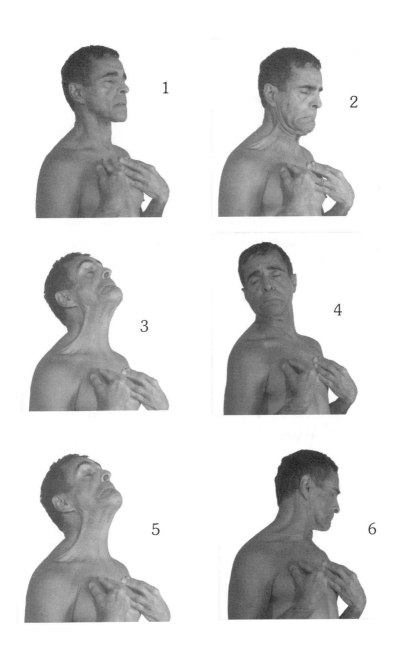

Section Six - Rejuvenation Exercises

<u>**Face & Neck**</u>

lateral neck stretch
(sirsha-matsyasana)

Standing with the feet about the width of the shoulders, and hooking the right hand on the left side of the head, tilt the head, chin facing forward, to the right shoulder, and place the left hand from the rear, on the inner part of the left thigh.

Begin resistance by drawing the right hand to the right, and pushing the left hand into the left. Hold for ten seconds, and repeat on the opposite side. Do only once per side. This works deep into the neck and shoulder.

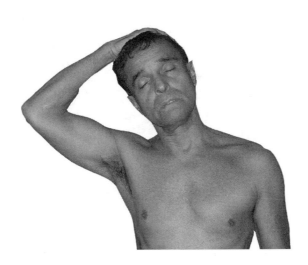

Section Six - Rejuvenation Exercises

half lotus
(ardha padmasana)

Sit on the floor with the legs straightened in front of the body. Bend the right leg drawing the foot in, toward the rear of the right thigh. Hook the right forearm from the inside under the right foreleg.

Lift the leg and place the left hand at the outer side of the right ankle. Raise the leg until a stretch is felt at the hip. Do not pull at all with the left hand up to this point. After the hip stretch is felt, draw the right foot in toward the head (to place the pressure lower on the thigh toward the knee, and somewhat at the ankle). This placement of the foot is accomplished with the left hand.

Keeping the right foot close to the body, lower it onto the left leg at the junction of the thigh and torso. The right heel should be at the center of the body, and the sole of the foot should face up. The right knee should rest on the floor.

Because of tautness at the inner thigh or at the hip or knee, the right knee might not touch the floor. If this is the case, practice the closed bow (dhanurasana), the half bow closed (ardha dhanurasana), and the cross bow (ardha dhanurasana). These three asanas (postures) will prepare the thigh for both the lotus and half lotus postures.

The lotus position and its' variations are quite significant in the practice of yoga. The placement of the feet and the pressure at the knee require explanation. If the position is not formed properly, undue pressure will be placed at areas which are not by design capable of supporting such pressure. Injury to the knee and ankle could result.

Never force the leg into the lotus position. Do not 'bounce' the leg up and down when holding the half-lotus posture. After placing the right leg in the half-lotus position, draw the left leg under the right, placing the left leg at the fold line under the right thigh. This is the half-lotus. Hold for as long as is comfortable. Reverse positions.

Section Six - Rejuvenation Exercises

Section Six - Rejuvenation Exercises

plow

classic version
halasana

Rise into the classic version of the shoulderstand (sarvangasana). Inhale and hold the position. Slowly lower the straight legs beyond the head toward the floor. When a stretch is felt at the rear of the thigh, begin to exhale, lowering the feet further.

Lower only so far as the body will allow with the legs straight. Do not bounce the legs down. During the movement place the hands at whichever point they feel most comfortable. On the floor between the feet and head, palm up, will probably be the most relaxing position. Otherwise, keep the hands at the hip area.

Breathe as little as possible while in the plow posture. Hold only as long as is comfortable. Inhale as the legs are raised. If the hands are between the head and feet, pressing the backs of the hands on the floor, will relieve some of the pressure from the abdomen and the low back, until the legs are strong enough to work alone.

When the legs are lowered be sure that they go no further than maintaining straight legs will allow. If the legs are allowed to bend as they lower, the straight legs to the floor position will never be reached.

This position may be repeated. This exercises the neck, shoulders, entire back, hips, gluteal region, rear of the leg and the lower abdomen. It also creates a visceral massage.

Section Six - Rejuvenation Exercises

Shoulderstand

Plow

Section Six - Rejuvenation Exercises

spinal twist
classic version
(ardha matsyendrasana)

Sit on the floor with the straightened legs together. Draw the right knee to the chest, placing the right foot on the floor at the buttocks. Cross the right foot to the outer left thigh. The right knee should be close to the chest, and the right foot flat on the floor with the toes forward.

Bend the left leg drawing the foot inward and under the right hip. Place the right hand behind the body, supporting the upper body with the right arm. The hand should be in line with the spine, and the fingertips to the rear.

Place the left elbow on the outer side of the right knee, and if possible grasp the top of the left knee with the left hand. Exhale and draw the tummy in a bit, turning to the right. A stretch should be felt at the outer right thigh. The ideal position for the shoulders is crossing directly through the center of the body.

If a problem is experienced in attempting to place the left elbow on the right knee and then grasp the foot, use the left arm to draw the right knee toward the left shoulder. Hold for a ten count and then release. Release first the forward arm and then the lower leg followed by the upper leg. Reverse. Do this once to begin with.

A spinal twist is created which as the student advances, will become more profound rising along the entire spine. The hip beneath the chin is also worked. Remember: the more flexible the spine, the younger the person; no matter what age he or she is chronologically.

Section Six - Rejuvenation Exercises

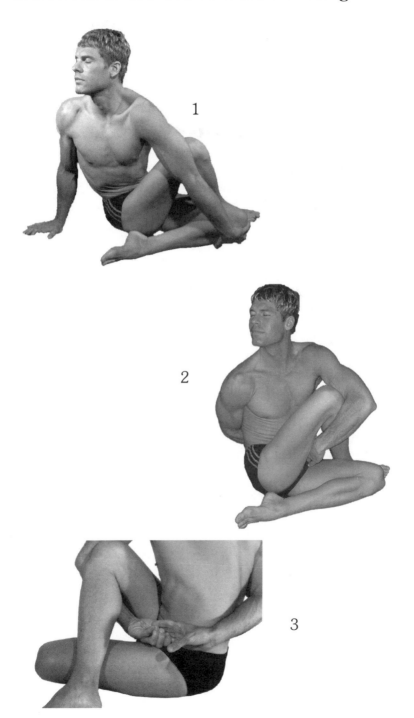

Section Six - Rejuvenation Exercises

triangle
(trikonasana)

Stand with the feet the width of the shoulders. Raise the left arm above the head. Touch the elbow to the head, and bend the arm dropping the hand behind the back.

Grasp the left elbow with the right hand. Exhale, and draw the left elbow toward the right shoulder. Be careful not to tilt the body as the elbow is drawn down. The elbow should be lowered until a stretch is felt at the left underarm. Draw the tummy in.

Holding this position and breathing as little as possible throughout the entire movement, tilt as far to the right as is comfortable. Be sure that the upper body does not bend forward. The upper elbow should be to the ceiling.

Hold this position for 20 seconds. Breathe as little as is possible, but as much as is needed. Rise and lower the arms. Repeat on the opposing side. This need be done but once. This works from the elbow to the knee as well as the latisimus dorsi, the low back and lower abdomen.

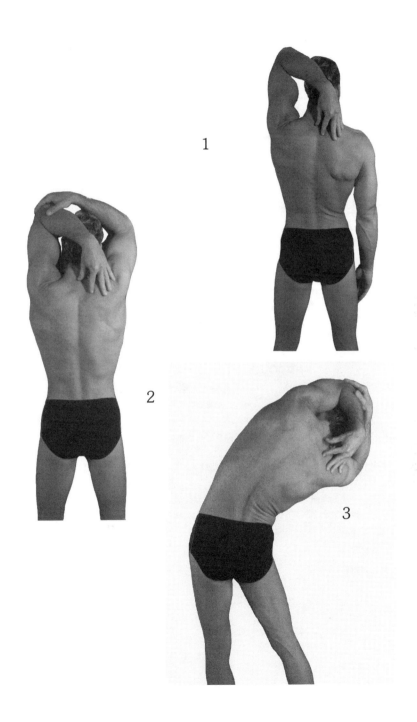

sitting split
(bhadrasana)

Sit on the floor with the knees to the chest and the feet at the center of the body. Lower the knees to the sides of the body. Place the feet sole to sole. Grasp just above the ankles, and place the elbows on the inner leg at the area of the knee.

Holding the feet in place by the ankle grip, relax the inner thigh and slowly apply pressure by pressing downward with the arms.

Lower as far as is comfortable and then relax the pressure allowing the knees to rise.

Repeat the process several times. With time the knees will lower to the floor. As you become more proficient in the asana, lower the upper body forward as the legs split.

This works the inner thigh, outer hip, buttocks, low back and abdomen. It has also been beneficial when used as a prenatal exercise.

Section Six - Rejuvenation Exercises

half pelvic
classic version
(ardha vajrasana)

Sit on the floor with both legs straightened in front of the body. Bend the right leg at the knee drawing the foot to the right hip. From this position with the palms down along side of the ankles, bend the left arm until the elbow rests on the floor.

If it is not too uncomfortable, lower the right elbow to the floor. By this point a stretch should be felt at the front thigh. Hold this position for a ten count, and then draw the bent leg from the center of the body, and sliding the elbows forward, bridge onto the head. Do this slowly and only if it can be accomplished comfortably and with the bent knee remaining on the floor.

Finally, if it is comfortably possible, lie completely flat on the back, with the right foot along side of the right hip. Hold for as long as is comfortable. Straighten the legs, sit erect, reverse positions, and hold for as long as is comfortable on the opposing side.

One side is generally more flexible than the other, so no holding time is given. This works the entire front of the leg (quadriceps), as well as the outer thigh and hip area, and the low abdomen.

With time, both legs may be worked at the same time. Do not rush this last step. A great exercise for patience.

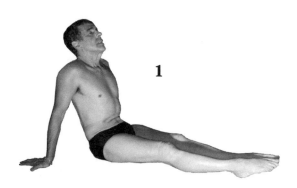

1

Section Six - Rejuvenation Exercises

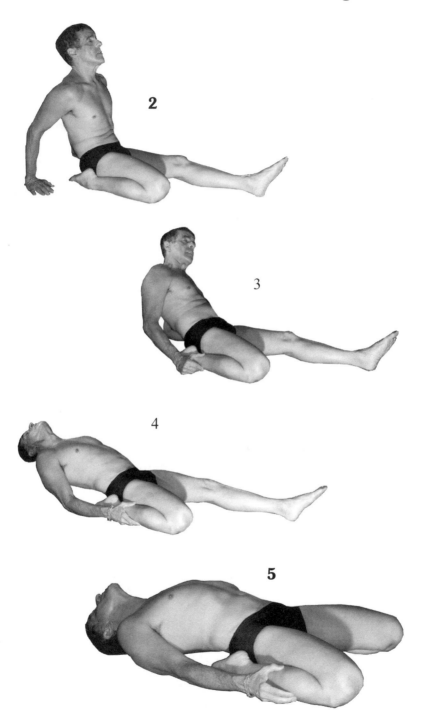

Section Six - Rejuvenation Exercises

frog
(mandukasana)

Kneeling with the knees the width of the shoulders, and the feet the width of the hips, exhale, bending forward and lower the hips to the floor, as the head is lowered forward.

Inhaling, raise the upper body and lower the seat close to the floor. Repeat the entire move. Be sure the toes curl in toward the center.

This will help to open the hip, knee and ankle areas of the body, as well as relax the body.

There is a common approach that teaches students to turn the toes outward. This is unsafe for the ligaments of the medial aspect of the knee and ankle area. This is a good asana for firming the instep of the foot, the front thigh, and the buttocks area.

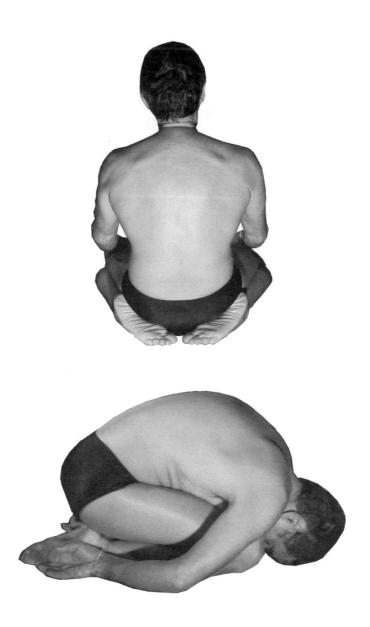

Section Six - Rejuvenation Exercises

head-knee
(janu-sirshasana)

Draw the left foot to the center of the body. Place the sole of the left foot against the inner thigh. The left knee should rest on the floor. Bend the right leg and grasp the great toe of the right foot with the index and middle fingers of the right hand.

Grasp the toe from the top, and place the elbow on the inside of the thigh. Draw the right knee to the chest. Straighten the right leg upward until a stretch is felt at the rear of the right thigh. The hand grip should of course be retained.

Place the left hand on the outer side of the right foot, from beneath and draw the foot in toward the chest. This position will place the pressure somewhat on the outer thigh and ankle. Releasing the left hand, straighten the leg upward, and then slowly lower the right foot to the floor. Do not drop the leg on the floor; set it there.

Exhale and lower the head to the knee. At first draw the upper body down by using the hands at the ankle or foot. As flexibility increases, attempt this posture without grasping with the hands. This works the low back, rear thigh and hip.

Section Six - Rejuvenation Exercises

Section Six - Rejuvenation Exercises

shoulder stretch
(hastasana)

Sitting with the legs straight out in front of the body with the hands palm down on the floor, and the fingertips facing the wall to the rear of you, bend the arms at the elbow.

From this position, inch the hands to the rear, maintain the bend at the elbow, until a stretch is felt at the front of the shoulder. If an undue stretch is felt at the inner wrist, either move the hands farther back or wider apart.

At this point tilt slightly to the left until a further stretch is felt at the front of the shoulder. From here bend the arm at the elbow, bending it farther backward. Be careful not to drop the elbow inward.

Hold this stretch for a ten count, and then rise to the center.

Repeat on the right side. At the center with hands still in place, and elbows as close as is comfortable, bend both elbows simultaneously, and when the stretch is felt at the front of the shoulders, raise the chin dropping the head backward, and hold for ten seconds. Rise to an arms straight position and relax.

This should not be attempted more than once. It is probably the most concentrated shoulder and arm exercise designed. Always do this slowly.

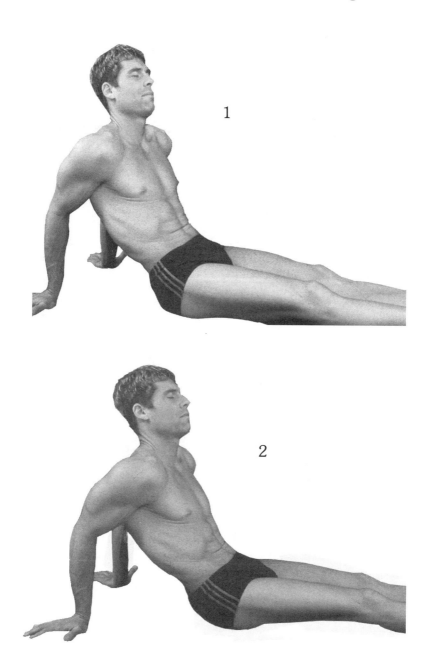

outer arm pull
hastasana

Hooking the hands at the level of the hip, and straightening the arms at the elbow, begin to resist, drawing them apart, being careful not to release the grip with the hands. Continue to resist for about ten seconds, and then (continuing resistance), slowly begin to bend the arms, drawing them up the front of the body, keeping them as close to the body as possible without touching the body.

Resist throughout the movement until the hands are raised above the head to the point where the arms are straightened again, and continue the pull ten seconds, then relaxing the pressure and retaining the grip, bend the arms at the elbow resting the hands on the head

After a comfortable rest, straighten the arms, reapplying the pressure, holding for ten seconds and then initiate movement again by slowly lowering the arms to the front of the body, being sure to maintain the arms as straight as is possible, as they arc out from the body. When the hands reach the hip, continue the resistance for ten seconds, and then relax the pressure releasing the grip.

Again hook the hands, raise the straightened arms up the front of the body, moving as slowly as possible, as they arc in a semi-circle, stretching them above and in back of the head, continuing the pull for ten seconds, then relax. Continue until the hands are at the elbows locked point again. After the hold, relax the pressure, release the grip, and shake the hands loosely.

This works every muscle in the arm from fingertip to shoulder, as well as the chest and upper back. Because of the tension created at the base of the neck, it will relieve pressure in that area. Unlike the asana or postures of hatha yoga, this is one of the karana kriya or isotonic or movement exercises. It works directly on six of the major meridians.

Section Six - Rejuvenation Exercises

locust

classic version

(salabasana)

Lying face down, with the palms under the thigh, place the feet the width of the shoulders.

Centering the weight on the chin, chest, shoulders and hands, inhale, raising both legs from the floor, and pushing down with the hands, raise the hips off the floor.

Have the legs as straight as possible. Hold for ten seconds. Exhale as the legs are lowered to the floor.

locust
(a variation)
salabhasana

Perform the classic version of the locust as described above. At the height of the holding position, with knees straight, draw the legs together touching the toes.

Hold for five seconds and then separate the legs as far apart as possible. Repeat.

This increases the intensity on the low back, tones the buttocks, hip and lateral thigh.

Do not perform this more than three times in succession.

half bridge

a variation

(ardha setu bhandasana)

Sitting upright on the floor, with the legs outstretched in front of the body, place the hands about a foot to the rear of the body palm down, with the fingertips facing to the side.

Rising on the toes, raise the hips, arching the body up. The apex of the arch should be at the hip area.

If the toes do not touch the floor, bend the knees so that they will. From this position raise the right leg from the floor, being sure that the leg remains straight. As the leg rises, raise the chin slowly, dropping the head backward. Inhale as the chin is raised.

Hold this position for a ten count. Lower the chin to the chest, and the leg to the floor, exhaling as they are lowered. Lower the hips and relax.

Repeat using the other leg. In order to maintain body balance, the leg which is supporting the body, should be in a vertical line with the body.

The areas worked with this asana are the lower rear thigh and the lower leg, front and rear. This will also relieve tension at the low back.

kneeling wheel
(ardha chakrasana)

Kneel down with the knees the width of the shoulders, the feet the width of the hip, and the seat on the floor. From this position form a fist with the hands, placing the fist on the soles of the feet.

Lean the shoulders in back of the line of the hip. That is, if a vertical line were drawn through the hip, the shoulders should be to the rear of this line.

Raise the hips from the heels of the feet. Arch as high as possible with the fists remaining on the feet. Without lowering the arch of the body, ride the hips farther forward, allowing the hands to leave the feet. Continue arching the body until the hips are over the knees. (Photo 3)

From this position place the hands at the front of the hip, and slowly arch backward, with the chin on the chest, until the hips are over the heels of the feet, and the head is touching the floor Rise back to position 3. At this point you may bend forward at the waist.

This may be repeated. The wider the knees, the easier the arch. However, if the knees are too wide control is diminished.

This is a great move for streamlining the body. It works the low back, the hip, the outer thigh, the front thigh, and the lower abdomen. This is one of the most important of the karana kriya exercises, and is a master move for developing abdominal control and raising the kundalini energy.

1

2

Section Six - Rejuvenation Exercises

Section Six - Rejuvenation Exercises

wheel
(classic version)
(chakrasana)

Lie on the back, with the feet at the hip, and the palms at the shoulders, with the fingers pointed toward the feet.

This is accomplished by raising the hands above the head, bending them at the elbow, and placing the palms on the floor.

Rising on the toes, place the feet as close to the shoulders as possible. Bridge onto the head, moving it as close to the feet as possible. Replace the hands under the shoulders. With the elbows facing the ceiling, arch the body, and then straighten the arms.

The body should now be supported on hands and toes. Lower and repeat. This works every muscle group at the front and back of the body, and will increase balance and control

This is another of the karana kriya exercises.

Section Six - Rejuvenation Exercises

wheel
(half diamond posture)
(ardha supta vajrasana)

Rise in the wheel, (as in the previous exercise), and placing the chin on the chest, maintain the elbows close together. Slowly bend the elbows, lowering the upper body to the floor. Maintain the chin on the chest, and with the elbows close, again straighten the arms, raising the body from the floor.

Repeat slowly and as many times as is comfortable. This is probably the best upper back exercise, next to the advanced balance moves. It also works the entire arm as well as the thigh and the chest in an unusual manner.

An internal massage is created on the kidney, liver and spleen. This is another of the karana kriya exercises.

Section Six - Rejuvenation Exercises

shoulderstand to bridge
(savanga-chakrasana)

In order to accomplish this version of the shoulderstand, you must first be able to attain a free arm shoulderstand, also known as a "ramrod" shoulderstand. (photo 1)

Separate the feet to about the width of the shoulders. Place the hands at the low back area, thumbs against the back. Generally, the finger side of the hand would be placed against the back for support. This version however, requires abdominal, low back and hip control. To demonstrate this, we use the thumbs as a guide (not to rest on them), rather than use the hands as a buttress.

From this point, contract at the area of the low back and lower abdomen at the same time. You must keep the hips high in order to do this properly. Bend your left leg, lowering it in the direction of the floor, away from your head. Keep the right leg high as a counter-balance. Be careful not to let the lowering left leg hit the floor, but instead, gently touch the floor and then slowly raise that same leg until it is above your head. At this point slowly lower the right leg, and in the same manner as the previous leg.

Eventually, this can be attempted with both legs simultaneously.

This is one of the karana kriya master moves.

Section Six - Rejuvenation Exercises

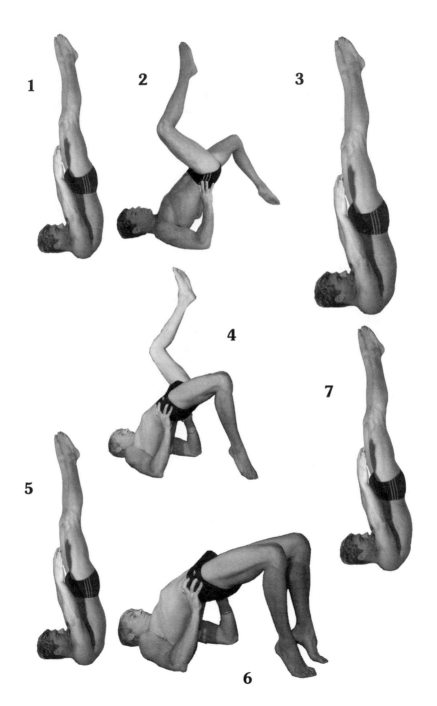

Section Six - Rejuvenation Exercises

tripod headstand
(trikona-sirshasana)

Kneel with the hips on the heels of the feet. Bend forward and rest the head on the floor in front of the knees, place the palms alongside of the feet. Fingertips should be in line with the toes.

Maintaining the head, hands and toes stationary, straighten the legs and raise the hips as high as is comfortable. The head should be set on it's crown (the very top), and not on the forehead. The elbows should be slightly bent.

Push down with the hands and gradually raise the legs. At first they may be bent and with time straightened. The weight is distributed between hands the head. Raise the legs slowly until the feet are above the head. Hold to assure balance, and then lower the legs slowly to the floor. The legs should be as straight as possible.

Be careful not to move the hips or rotate at all on the head. The hips should not move beyond the point of the shoulders. If the head feels at all uncomfortable, place a small pillow or blanket under the head.

This will aid in developing balance as well as strengthen the low back, abdomen, legs, arms and neck It is a basic balance. This is the easiest of the headstand variations to hold. The power and control developed at the abdomen, low back and neck, will prepare the body for more difficult variations. This is another of the karana kriya.

Section Six - Rejuvenation Exercises

1

2

3

4

Section Six - Rejuvenation Exercises

endurance, energy, stamina & strength: are developed through a combination of flexibility and contractility along with a sound nutritional and cleansing program.

balance:

shoulderstand
(a variation no arms)
(savangasana)

Rise into the shoulderstand using either the "tuck" (knee to chest) or "pike" (straight legs) positions. Stretch the legs high toward the ceiling, placing the weight on the neck and high on the shoulders.

Lower the straight legs a few inches toward the head, by bending at the waist, and slowly remove the hands from the hips, supporting the weight slightly with the elbows.

Lower the legs a fraction more until the pressure is relieved from the elbows, and slowly raise the arms placing the hands on the front thigh just above the knee.

To counteract any over extension of the legs, a slight pressure may be employed by the hands on the thighs. Breath as little as possible when doing this asana. The balance is delicate. In all the variations of the shoulderstand, maintain the posture for as long as is comfortable. This may be held for several minutes.

Tuck

Pike

headstand
(sirshasana)
(classic version)

To many this seems to be the essence of hatha yoga. A new student will always ask if he or she can learn a headstand. Any who is structurally normal and not excessively heavy can hold this balance.

Begin by kneeling on a small mat of blanket. Set the hips on the heels of the feet. Bend forward and place the front of the crown of the head on the floor. Clasp the hands at the back of the head. It will be better to overlap the fingers rather than interlock them. Be sure that the knees are together. Draw the knees right up to the eye sockets. Place the elbows in close to the legs. Arch the foot rather than stand on the toes. Place the weight on the elbows. Be sure that the body is as comfortable as possible. Relax the low back and be careful not to re-arrange any part of the body from the placement described.

Keeping in mind that when the tail of the spine (hip area), is above the shoulders, and the weight is on the elbows and forearm, that the balance will be attained. Raise the hips slowly by straightening the legs at the knee until a pull is felt at the rear of the leg. Caution must be used to maintain body position with the weight on the elbows, and the hands, head and toes, stationary. Breathe as little as possible. Draw the tummy in, and exhale slightly. Remove one foot from the floor, and draw the knee to the chest. Remove the other foot giving as little push as possible, and bring the lower knee to the upper. The hips should begin to rise, almost displaying a caution. If the above is followed to the letter, the hips should cease motion   when situated above the shoulders.

Hold this position for a bit to assist the balance. A sensation of possibly toppling will be felt if this is done properly; and yet the body will paradoxically remain in balance. This feeling is due to the fact that when the body is in balance, it can topple in any direction.

Section Six - Rejuvenation Exercises

Section Six - Rejuvenation Exercises

This is simply because balance is the fine point between two points of imbalance, forward and backward, or right and left. Consequently, the weight must constantly (and yet almost imperceptibly) be shifted from elbows to hands and back to elbows again.

The body weight should at no time be placed directly on the head while attempting or holding this asana. The cervical vertebrae (those vertebra of the neck), are not designed by nature to support the weight of the body from shoulders to feet; especially if one weighs more than natures' design has intended.

The head should merely be set into the cupped hands with the hands situated at the occipital curve (prominent bump) at the rear of the head.

To lower the body, reverse the steps by resisting with the elbows, and placing a bit more weight on the hands, slowly lowering the hips and placing the feet on the floor. Lower the feet to the hips. Relax.

Holding a headstand in this tucked position is the very essence of a headstand. As confidence is gained, the legs may be straightened slowly to the ceiling. When this posture is first attempted, it might be helpful to try it in a corner of the room. Try not to rest the hips against the wall. A part of learning to balance is to be inverted. The inversion of the body, coupled with a touch of confidence, will accomplish wonders in overcoming tension, the "my head is about to explode" feeling, and the lack of a sense of balance which is normal when first inverted. May the student be cautioned however, that the wall if used should be a guide and not a buttress. The idea of using a wall is to stop if possible just before contact is made with the wall.

The hips should not arch causing an abdominal protrusion. This is a common error. Unfortunately, it is at times taught. If the body does arch, too much pressure may be placed on the low back and cervicals (vertebrae of the neck).

After lowering from the balance, sit up for a moment to allow the equilibrium to return. Do not hold for more than fifteen to thirty seconds at the beginning. Each time it is held, the balance should be maintained for as long as is comfortable. Balance can be controlled from any moveable point of the body. The eyes play a special role in this. They should concentrate on a spot approximately body length away from the head. If the eyes roam, so also will the balance.

The benefits of the headstand are so numerous and far reaching, that to list even a portion of them sounds to the

Section Six - Rejuvenation Exercises

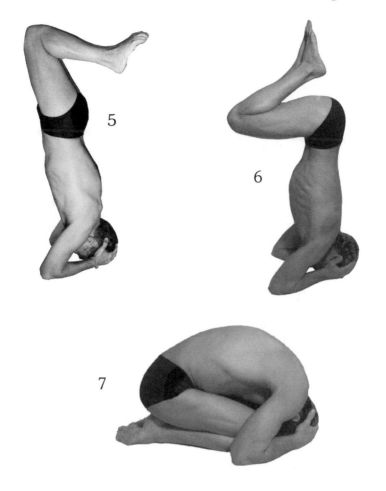

novice as gross exaggeration. The claims of many authorities as well as innumerable students range from a tendency to relieve headache, nervousness, insomnia, indigestion, congested throat, asthma, constipation, eye, ear, nose, liver and spleen diseases in their initial stages, to uterine and ovarian disorders, and seminal weakness. It is a beneficial tonic for the heart, a promoter of good circulation, benefitting the entire nervous system, stimulating also the endocrine system.

It has particular benefit if done before going to bed at night, and upon arising in the morning. If you are sleepy, it tends to wake you up, and if you are excited it tends to make you drowsy by relaxing the system.

Section Six - Rejuvenation Exercises

crow
(classic version)
kakasana

Standing on the feet, squat and place the palms on the floor below the shoulders. Spread the fingers wide. Rise onto the toes and place the inner part of the leg just below the knee on top of the elbows. Cup the hands in the same way that you would crimp the feet when standing on the toes. Up to this point the eyes have been staring at the apex of the equilateral triangle formed by the two hands and the third point being formed by where the eyes are looking.

The distance from hand to the eye spot is the same as from hand to hand, approximately the width of the shoulders. Move the eyes down slowly until the body tilts to a point where the feet begin to leave the floor. Do not attempt to kick the feet from the floor. Constantly resist with the fingers as the body tilts forward.

When the toes leave the ground, stop the eye movement. The eyes should remain at this point raising them only when you want to lower the feet back to the floor. The knees must be kept in close to the elbows. The spine should remain rigid throughout. This is a modified handstand. Balance will be improved. The arms will be strengthened.

An advanced variation of this is to place both knees on one side, (fig. 3) spotting on the hand on the same side as the knees.

This is also a coordination exercise.

Section Six - Rejuvenation Exercises

peacock
(mayurasana)

Place the palms on the floor. Point the fingertips toward the feet. Set the elbows just above and on the inside of the hips. Exhale slightly and place the forehead on the floor. Raise the legs. Point the toes. Raise the head. If the eyes roam, so will the balance.

The Peacock Posture creates a greater abdominal massage than almost any other conditioning exercise. The sole exceptions being the abdominal control exercises (uddiyana bhandha and nauli). Balance of course is also improved.

Section Six - Rejuvenation Exercises

kneeling half moon
(ardha chakrasana)
a variation

Kneel down on the right knee and arch the right foot. Place the left heel on the floor below and about five to six inches in front of the left knee. Bend the left knee riding the hips forward until a stretch is felt at the front of the right thigh.

At this point extend the right leg (raising the right knee from the floor), and raise the chest and arms aching the back slightly. Hold for ten and then slowly lower the knee to the floor. Repeat and then reverse.

This is marvelous for firming the front thigh and toning the hip area. It is an activator of the sexual drive, and will tend to alleviate constipation as will any knee to chest positions.

wheel
a variation
(ardha supta vajrasana)

     Rise into the wheel and placing the chin on the chest (maintain the elbows close together). Slowly bend the elbows, lowering the upper back to the floor. Maintain the chin on the chest, and with the elbows close, again straighten the arms, raising the body from the floor. Repeat slowly, but as many times as comfortable.

     This is probably the best upper back exercise next to the advanced balance moves. It also works the entire arm as well as thigh and the chest, in an unusual manner. An internal massage is created on the kidney, liver and spleen. Another of the karana kriya series.

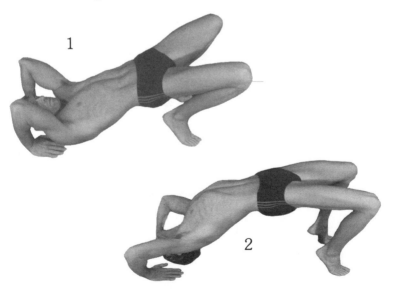

Section Six - Rejuvenation Exercises

eagle headstand
a classic variation
(garuda-sirshasana)

Enter the headstand as on page. The following is an advanced variation of the classic headstand.

In this asana/karana kriya exercise, leg positions should be applied separately. With the feet together, bend the right leg placing the rear of the right thigh on the front of the left thigh. In order to do this the right knee must be inferior to the left knee. Bend the left leg hooking the right foot to the rear of the left foreleg.

It will help to over extend the hips toward the rear.

This increases balance, flexibility and mind/body control. It is one of the twelve Master Moves of hatha (physical) yoga.

1

2

3

classic headstand

eagle left leg in front

eagle right leg in front

Section Six - Rejuvenation Exercises

sun salutation

soorya namaskar

This is called the sun series or sun salutation, because in ancient times it was done in the morning to honor the sun as it rose. As with most series in yogic lore this has twelve counts or movements. Each angle created by the body represents a different constellation. There are many versions of this karana kriya exercise series, but the one presented here we feel is the most beneficial.

Begin by standing with the feet together.

1. Inhale raising the arms above the head. Reach up, forward and down; exhaling on the way down.

2. Place the palms on the floor, or grasp the toes.

3. Set the right leg backward until the rear thigh (right) is stretched. The left leg is bent, the chest is high, and the back is arched. Inhale as the back arches. The right knee should not touch the floor.

4. Raise the hands from the floor and raise the upper body, arching the back further as the arms rise. The palms should be placed together, or with thumbs hooked to the ceiling. Inhale slightly, and hold to assure balance. Lower the arms and place the hands on the floor (4a).

5. Place the left foot alongside of the right. Bend the elbows and lower the body to the floor, exhaling.

6. The forehead, hands, chest, knees and toes, should touch the floor. Lower the hips and arch the feet, raising the chest and straightening the arms. The body should now be in the cobra position.

7. Inhale as the cobra is attained. Exhale and lower the body. Raise the chin and hip from the floor. Rise onto the toes.

8. Raise the hips higher and push the chest from the floor. The body should now be in the pike position (supported only on the hands and feet or the fingers and toes). Some women will have to modify the upward rise when first attempting the sun

Section Six - Rejuvenation Exercises

1

3

2

3a

4

5

Section Six - Rejuvenation Exercises

series. Tuck the chin into the chest and stretch the tail high, exhaling.

9. Draw the right knee up to the chest, and set the foot on the floor.

10. Raise the hands, chest and arms; arching the back as the body rises. A stretch should be felt at the front of the left thigh. Hold to assure balance. Inhale as the upper body rises.

11. Lower the hands to the floor Draw the left knee to the chest, and set the foot on the floor along side of the right foot. The knees are still bent. Grasp the ankles with the hands, set the head on the knees, and maintaining the head there, Straighten the legs, exhaling.

12. Rise to a standing position, hands at the thigh area and relax.

The basic rules of inhaling when the upper and lower body move apart, and exhaling when they come together, applies in this combination. This is a classic karana kriya isotonic yoga series, usually viewed as an asana, clearly it involves movement.

Section Six - Rejuvenation Exercises

10

11

12

Section Six - Rejuvenation Exercises

moon series

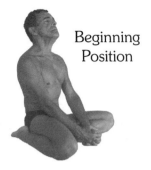

Beginning
Position

(chandra namaskar)

This series was prescribed to be practiced in the evening. The Sun series exercises all those muscles that can extend *anteriorly* and *posteriorly*. The Moon series works those muscles that extend and contract laterally and medially. This is another of the *karana kriya*.

Sit with the left foot at the center of the body, and the right foot at the lateral hip. Interlace the fingers at the front of the body.

1. Inhale, raising the arms above the head.

2. Exhaling, lowering the chest, hands, elbows and forehead to the floor, at a point central to the knees.

3. Inhale, as you raise the upper body, arms above the head.

4. Exhale as you lower the upper body to the left knee grasping the knee, elbows to the floor and head to the knee.

5. Rise to an erect position, inhale, hands overhead.

6. Tilt to the right, until you feel a stretch at the left underarm.

*7.*Go forward to the right knee, exhaling. Grasp the knee with both hands, Exhale lowering the chest to thigh, elbows to the floor, and head to the knee.

8. Rise to an erect position, arms above the head.

9. Lower the arms to the side.

10. Reach to the rear of the body, grasping the toes of the right foot with the left hand. Lower the chest to the left thigh. Lift the right knee and thigh off the floor, turning the front thigh to the floor and pushing the foot away from the torso, as you raise the chest. Do not to touch the right leg to the floor as you extend.

11. Lower the leg to the floor and arms to the side.

12. Inhale, as you raise the torso.There are other variations of **chandrasana namaskar**, the moon series, but this is the most comprehensive.

Again the twelve counts of the series are symbolic of the twelve constellations and the major energy channels of the human body.

Section Six - Rejuvenation Exercises

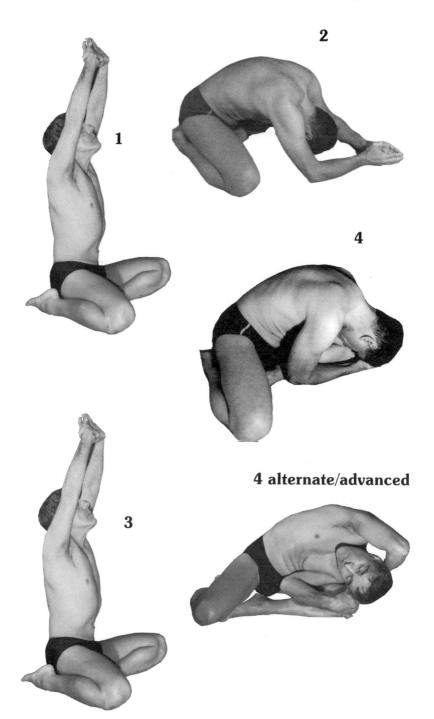

1

2

3

4

4 alternate/advanced

Section Six - Rejuvenation Exercises

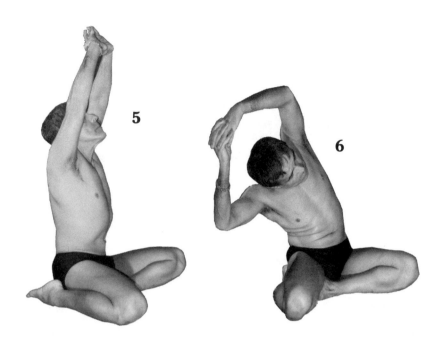

Section Six - Rejuvenation Exercises

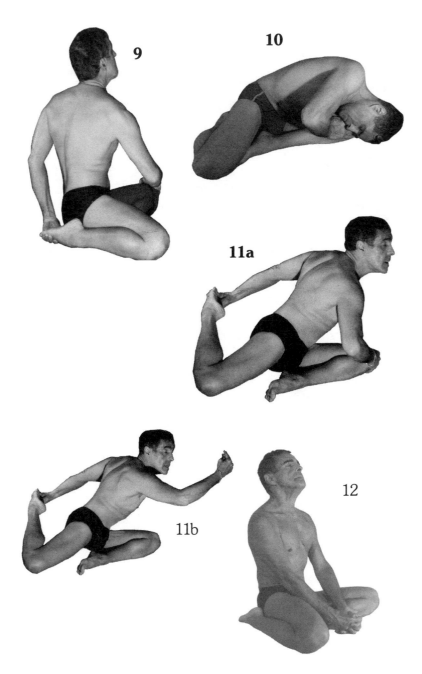

Section Six - Rejuvenation Exercises

abdominal uplift
(*uddiyana bhandha*)

The following exercise is not a breathing exercise as such nor is it an asana, which it is often referred to as. It is a bhandha or contraction exercise. There are three main bhandha in hatha yoga. The Sanscrit term "uddiyana" means to "fly upward".

In execution it creates a hole or vacuum, as it is more commonly called, at the area of the abdominal cavity. This is a marvelous exercise for energizing the body when fatigued.

It is performed by exhaling as completely as possible, and maintaining the exhalation. From this point begin to draw inward and upward the lower abdominal area. This means all the abdominal muscles beneath the line that runs just above the navel.

When this motion is first attempted, it will probably feel awkward and to some even impossible, but it is quite simple, and generally is accomplished within a few minutes of the first attempt at it.

It is more easily accomplished by bending forward at the waist and by bending the knees slightly, and placing the hands high on the thighs and applying pressure. This is another of the karana kriya, or control exercises.

Section Six - Rejuvenation Exercises

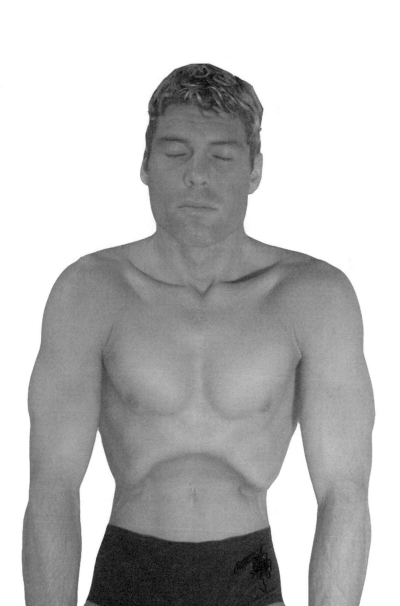

Section Six - Rejuvenation Exercises

nauli kriya
(abdominal manipulation)
a cleansing & control movement

This is one of the yogic kriya. This exercise is one of the most important exercises you can ever learn. Uddiyana bhandha must be accomplished with ease if this is to be done at all.

Stand with the feet comfortably apart. Exhale and bend forward slightly, creating the abdominal vacuum (uddiyana bhandha) (photo 1). Place the hands on the thighs causing the central abdominal muscles (rectus abdominus) to contract and consequently stand forth (photo 2). The further manipulation shall be explained separately.

The lungs take up the general area of the chest cavity, and in the space beneath this is the abdominal cavity. Most of our readers have heard the expression, "Nature abhors a vacuum". When we exhale, a vacuum is created in the chest cavity. To compensate for this vacuum, the abdominal contents (intestines and the other organs), rise through a natural uplift into the area of the chest cavity. By conscious mental discipline the abdominal contents are drawn further into the chest area. This motion creates the uddiyana bhandha (photo 1).

Pressing on the thighs will draw the abdomen further in. A bit of mental discipline will be required to then contract the central abdominal muscles (abdominal recti). There are two methods for abdominal manipulation. The first is

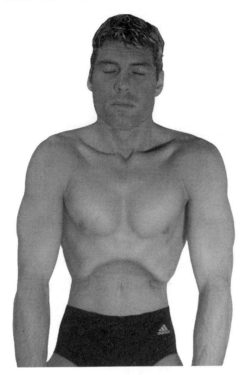

1

2

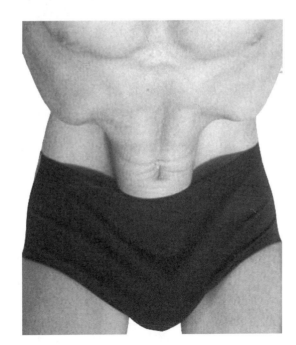

Section Six - Rejuvenation Exercises

mechanical and the second is mental control. When the hands are pressed on the thighs, the abdomen will contract somewhat. When the nauli is first learned, hand pressure will be required. When the hand pressure is released, the abdominal recti will rise again.

After contracting the abdominal recti, relax the pressure with the right hand. The right side of the recti should relax and rise into the abdomen (photo 3). Reapply the pressure with the right hand, and that side of the recti will drop forward again. Relax the left hand pressure, and the left recti will rise (photo 4). Reapply the pressure and the muscle will drop forward again. This contraction and relaxation is repeated alternating between the right and left hands (photos 3&4 combined).

A "jerky" motion will be found, but the abdominal roll will be accomplished. The above described method is mechanical manipulation. With time, power will reach the point where the muscles can be controlled with less hand manipulation. Gradually the flow will become rhythmic, and the alternating pressures with the hands will be unnecessary. Neurologically, this is called **neuro-bio-taxis**.

The abdominal control should be worked from left to right and from right to left. It should be held in the center, to the right, to the center, and then to the left, and back to the center. The central isolation of the muscles is called madyama in the Sanskrit. The left contraction is called vama nauli, and the right contraction is dakshina nauli.

This is the greatest abdominal exercise we have ever encountered. Unlike calisthenic sit-ups and leg raises, which work body weight against the abdomen, the nauli movements develop the abdomen by causing the muscles to develop themselves. This action is totally unique to yoga.

Section Six - Rejuvenation Exercises

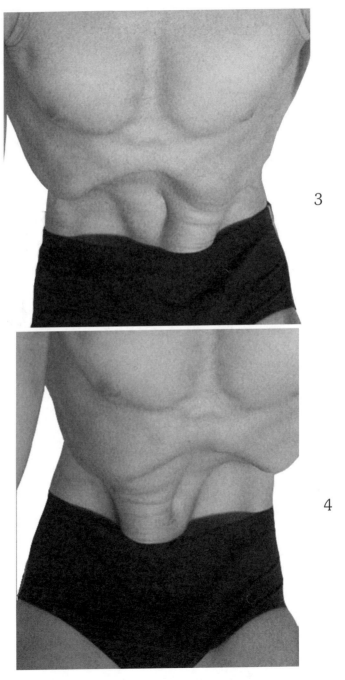

3

4

Section Six - Rejuvenation Exercises

This is the essence of physical development and control. In reality what is occurring is a process known as **neuro-bio-taxis**, as mentioned above. This is a neurological term that will be found only in a medical dictionary. It is the method by which the yogis are able to develop mastery over the processes of the human body. It is developed through mentally concentrating on the contraction and relaxation of a particular area of the body, and through repetition, gradually, an axonic growth actually sprouts from the central nervous system to grow to the area being concentrated on, and that area then comes under conscious control.

The resulting nauli exerciser actually creates a visceral massage, contracting and relaxing the tissues of the large and small intestines, the stomach, pancreas, spleen, thymus, liver, gall bladder, kidneys, urinary bladder, heart and lungs. In the process of doing this, it also activates an adrenal release. The result is a smooth flowing yet boundless energy, and an inexpensive, yet natural (and still legal) "high".

Section Six - Rejuvenation Exercises

Acupoints

362 You're Never Too Old To Become Young Acupoints

This section is on acupoints. Acupoints are the same as acupuncture points but instead of using needles to apply the technique, finger pressure is used. This is a very ancient and traditional approach to healing using touch.

We have chosen several treatments we felt would be helpful to our readers, as you travel along your path, to a totally natural health plan.

In applying pressure, use the spatulate side of the finger or thumb (the face of the fingertip), rather than the conical or tip (point) aspect of the finger or thumb.

Press until the spot feels slightly uncomfortable, and then massage in a circular motion several times. This may be done for several minutes. Work on each of the points for each chart. The healthier your body becomes, the more effective will be the results. Repeat this procedure several times daily.

We hope this is a great adjunct to your new lifestyle changes. Be patient and treat yourself with lots of love. Treat yourself as if you are the most important asset you have. After all, aren't you.

in Peace and Health always and in all ways,

David and Shawn, your authors

Acupoints

Allergies

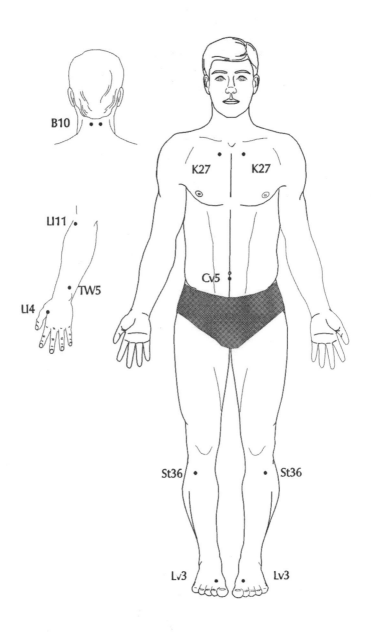

B10

K27   K27

LI11

Cv5

TW5

LI4

St36   St36

Lv3   Lv3

Acupoints

Asthma - Bronchitis

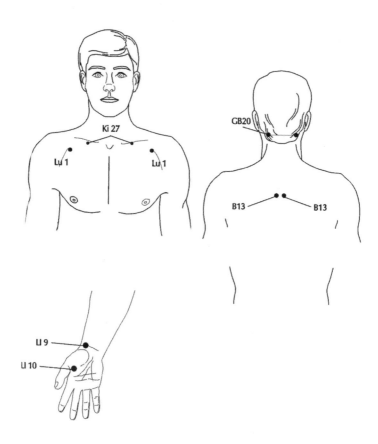

Acupoints

Backache

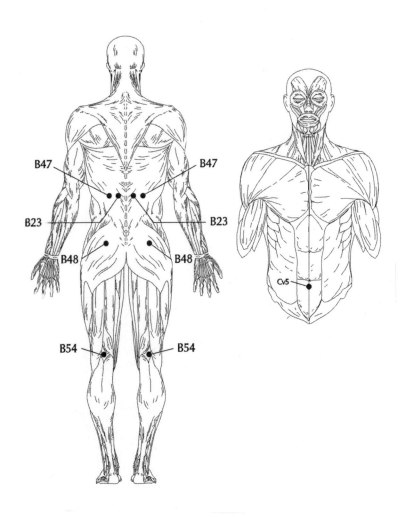

B47   B47

B23   B23

B48   B48

Cv5

B54   B54

Acupoints

Concentration

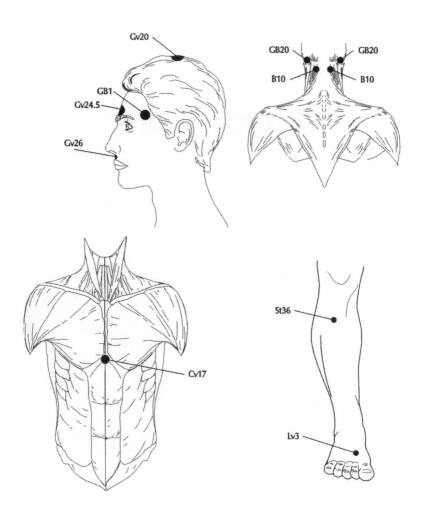

Acupoints

Constipation

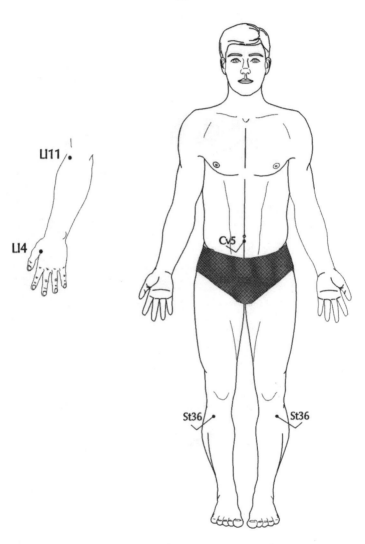

Depression

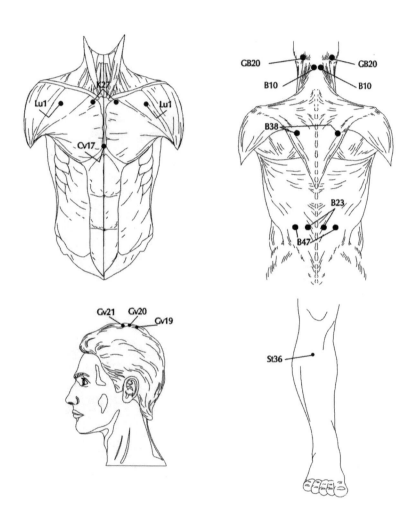

Acupoints

Hot Flashes

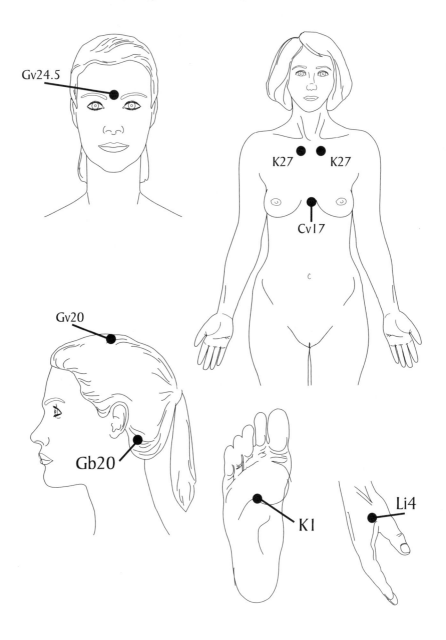

Gv24.5

K27   K27

Cv17

Gv20

Gb20

K1

Li4

Acupoints

www.perfecthealthnow.com

Channeled by Rt.Rev. David John Carmos

The
ESSENE
MASTER

BOOK
&
COMPACT
disc

The return journey of
yesuah to the holy land

www.perfecthealthnow.com

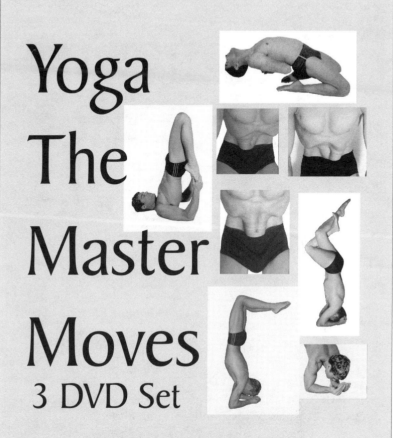

Yoga The Master Moves
3 DVD Set

David John Carmos
Dr. Shawn Miller

Featuring the 12 Master Moves of
Hatha Yoga

www.yogathemastermoves.com

www.perfecthealthnow.com

Eating
Vegan
Just
for the
Health
of It

www.perfecthealthnow.com

Index

Index

Index

Index

Index